100 THINGS SUCCESSFUL LEADERS DO

LITTLE LESSONS IN LEADERSHIP

100 THINGS SUCCESSFUL LEADERS DO

LITTLE LESSONS IN LEADERSHIP

NIGEL CUMBERLAND

First published by Nicholas Brealey Publishing in 2020
An imprint of John Murray Press
A division of Hodder & Stoughton Ltd,
An Hachette UK company

6

A CIP catalogue record for this title is available from the British Library

Trade Paperback ISBN 9781529353310

Ebook ISBN 9781529353334

Typeset by Cenveo® Publisher Services.

Printed and bound in Great Britain by Clays Ltd, Elcograf S.p.A.

John Murray Press policy is to use papers that are natural, renewable and recyclable products and made from wood grown in sustainable forests. The logging and manufacturing processes are expected to conform to the environmental regulations of the country of origin.

John Murray Press
Carmelite House
50 Victoria Embankment
London EC4Y 0DZ

Nicholas Brealey Publishing
Hachette Book Group
Market Place, Center 53, State Street
Boston, MA 02109, USA

www.nicholasbrealey.com

This book is dedicated to my son, Zeb, my step-daughter, Yasmine, and to all those wishing to become outstanding leaders. May each of you find your own unique paths to leadership success.

'If your actions inspire others to dream more, learn more, do more and become more, you are a leader.'

– John Quincy Adams

Contents

About the author

Nigel Cumberland is the co-founder of The Silk Road Partnership, a leading global provider of executive coaching and leadership training solutions to some of the world's leading organizations. He has lived and worked in locations as diverse as Hong Kong, Glasgow, Budapest, Santiago, Guatemala City, Kuala Lumpur, London and Shanghai, gaining experiences and wisdom that have helped teach him what it takes to succeed in life.

Previously, Nigel worked as a multinational finance director with Coats plc, as well as for some of the world's leading recruitment firms including Adecco. He is a Fellow of the UK's Chartered Institute of Management Accountants. He co-created an award-winning recruitment firm based in Hong Kong and China, which he later sold to Hays plc. Educated at Cambridge University, UK, Nigel is an extensively qualified executive coach and leadership training professional.

He is the author of a large number of self-help and leadership books, among the most recent of which are: *100 Things Millionaires Do: Little Lessons in Creating Wealth* (Nicholas Brealey Publishing, 2019), *The Ultimate Management Book* (John Murray Learning, 2018), *100 Things Successful People Do: Little Exercises for Successful Living* (John Murray Learning, 2016), *Secrets of Success at Work: 50 Techniques to Excel* (Hodder & Stoughton, 2014), *Finding and Hiring Talent in a Week* (John Murray Learning, 2016) and *Leading Teams in a Week* (John Murray Learning, 2016).

Nigel is married to a wonderful woman named Evelyn, who spends her time as an artist. He has two inspiring children – a son, Zeb, and a stepdaughter, Yasmine.

Introduction

'Everything you have thought, done and said in your life has prepared you to become the leader you are today.'

Are you ready to kick-start your leadership journey? Well done, you have picked up the perfect book to serve as your guide. This book will help you master the key habits, skills and behaviours to enable you to excel in whatever types of leadership roles you take on.

Leadership comes in all shapes and sizes from leading a voluntary group in the evenings, managing a children's sports team at weekends, or heading a large and busy family, to taking on a managerial or supervisory role for the first time, launching your own start-up business with only yourself to manage, or as CEO of one of the world's largest corporations.

It doesn't matter how little or large, how trivial or important. Leadership is leadership. The art of inspiring, organizing and motivating your kids at home is not a million miles away from successfully being a Board Chairperson of one of the largest listed groups in the world. It's so fantastic that you're reading this book and that you want to strengthen your leadership knowledge and capabilities. The world is awaiting you to turn into the most amazing leader you're capable of.

The need for better leadership is everywhere:

- Governments struggle to find focus, to lead not just their communities and countries, but also themselves. So many political leaders struggle to even complete their full terms of office.
- Companies of all sizes are facing so much disruption, complexity and competition that their management teams are stretched to perform well.
- Sports teams struggle to find consistency, with so many teams churning through coaches and trainers.
- Public sectors are challenged in part by a lack of funds to cope with issues such as weak schooling systems and hospitals at breaking point.
- Scandals remind us of weak leadership in our own communities – from the church in crisis through to family units breaking up.

When you think of a successful leader, who comes to mind?

Perhaps it's those in very visible, formal and often very large leadership roles such as Sir Richard Branson or Donald Trump. Perhaps you're inspired by those in smaller but still crucial roles such as your boss, former headteacher, head of your local council, your MP or congresswoman, your business partner or spouse. The 100 lessons in this book are designed to turn you into the type of leader that others will admire and want to learn from too.

I've coached hundreds of leaders working in organizations as diverse as the United Nations, World Bank Group, global banks and multinationals through to local tech start-ups, governments, schools and NGOs such as Teach for India. I've heard every leadership aspiration and dream you can imagine. I've listened to all the challenges and difficulties you'll likely face when taking on a leadership role.

The main lesson I have picked up is a simple one - too many people fail to work on all aspects of their leadership toolbox leaving them with underutilized skills and strengths, while hanging onto weaknesses which hold them back. Not you... working through this book is your opportunity to sit down and think about yourself, giving you time to ask yourself how you want to develop and grow as a leader, to create followers and future leaders, and to explore how you want to remembered by those you have led.

Treat this book as your trusted companion. Through 100 short chapters, you'll learn to make sense of the pieces you need to slot together to achieve your leadership ambitions. You'll explore what leadership means to you through topics including:

- Self-leadership
- Your motivations
- Leadership styles
- Leadership mindsets and behaviours

- Thinking and communicating as a leader
- Motivating and inspiring followers
- Dealing with leadership challenges
- Leading through change
- Creating leaders and handing over.

How to use this book

Every chapter in this book features a new idea that will help you get closer to your goals. In each chapter, the ideas are introduced and explained on the first page and the second page features exercises and activities, some small and some large, for you to start doing today.

Don't overlook the activities. The tasks you've been set have been specifically designed to give you the optimal mindset, habits, skills, relationships and behaviours needed to maximize your chances of leadership success. Some of them will surprise you, some will challenge you, others will seem simple and obvious. All of them are important in building the portfolio of skills you need to become a talented leader. Completing them will set you on the path to developing a leadership mindset and a leader-focused 'to do' list. These things aren't easy to achieve and few people are willing to invest the required time and effort. Successful leaders do.

Who am I to talk about successful leaders?

This book draws on the wisdom I have gained from coaching and mentoring leaders from all over the world for the past 20 years. From global CEOs to struggling entrepreneurs, through to leaders in the public sector and charities to first-time managers just starting out on their leadership careers, all of them have something to share about the journey of becoming an outstanding leader. Their experiences combine with my own wisdom gained through some incredibly personal leadership highs and lows.

UNDERSTAND YOUR MOTIVATIONS

'Some people spend their entire lives looking to be leaders. For others, leadership is thrust on them even when it's the last thing they're looking for.'

Think about a time you've accepted leadership responsibility. What made you agree to it and would you be willing to take on that responsibility again? Chances are you accepted the role because of a combination of reasons, some of which come from within you, pushing you to put your hand up to lead, some of which come from external factors, like the situations you face or pressure from other people, pulling you to take charge.

When coaching experienced leaders, I ask them why they became leaders and many of their replies will resonate with you:

Reasons pushing you	Reasons pulling you
• I like to take charge. • I hate passively doing nothing. • I don't enjoy being led by others. • Somebody had to do it. • I wanted a higher salary, so accepted the leadership opportunity. • As an eldest sibling, I have always been a leader. • I can't stand taking orders. • I love helping other people. • I want to make changes and felt this was possible through leading.	• Nobody else was leading the project, so I stepped in. • My senior colleagues pleaded with me to apply for the vacant management position. • As a woman, I was encouraged to take on the role as part of a gender diversity drive. • I was under a lot of peer pressure. • I had no choice as I was the only suitable person. • I wanted to say 'no' but was afraid to turn down the promotion.

To be a successful leader, you have to understand *why* you've taken on leadership responsibilities. You may not like the reasons, it might have been all pull and no push, but by properly understanding your motivations, you can more successfully decide how you'll take on and excel in a leadership role.

Put it into action 1

Are you a natural leader or follower? Either way, you may need to adjust your natural instincts to get the best out of yourself.

Control the obsessive need to lead

The things that push you to want to lead are your internal drivers made up of your personality, ego, motivations and inner needs. If you always feel compelled to take the lead, it can indicate that you're an ambitious person who will always step up when the opportunity arises, but it's not always a good thing. This impulse can lead you to take on leadership responsibilities before you're ready or capable. You risk failing simply because you weren't willing to wait until you had more experience.

Overcome the reluctance to lead

You may face the opposite problem and have no wish to lead and no inclination to stand out. That's fine as long as you manage to avoid leadership roles, but a big problem when you have responsibility thrust on you. It's never a good idea to wait until you've been pushed into the swimming pool before learning to swim, so take the opportunity to read up on topics that you're not so comfortable with in advance, and make a mental decision to be more assertive in overcoming your worries.

Don't be bullied into accepting roles

Even the best leaders say no to new tasks and responsibilities now and again. For sure, there can be persuasive pull factors involved, but never be afraid to upset other people who are pushing you. Decide whether you feel ready and whether you want the additional responsibilities and accompanying recognition before accepting anything.

KNOW YOURSELF

'It can be uncomfortable looking deeply at yourself in the mirror, reflecting and acting on what's staring back at you.'

Understanding who you are is the first step to being able to lead others. This connection between knowing yourself and leading others is based upon what I refer to as four truths:

1. To truly understand another human being, you must first know yourself.
2. To successfully lead someone, you must understand who they are and what drives them.
3. Leadership ability is built on a foundation of being able to lead yourself.
4. Successful self-leadership is only possible when you understand yourself.

These four connections are shown visually below.

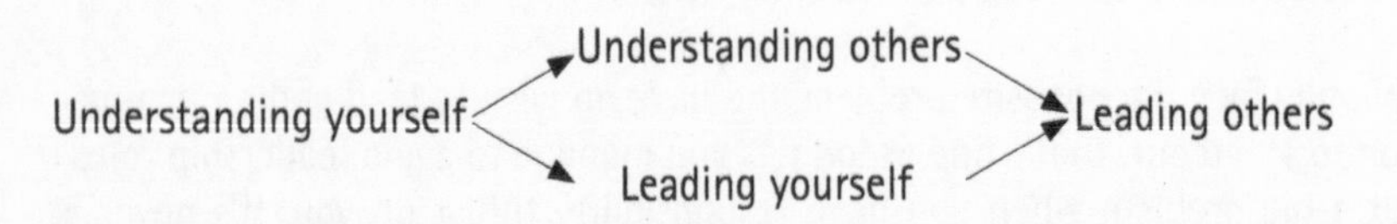

This chapter focuses on the first of these, with later chapters exploring the other three. We all think we know ourselves well, but few people truly do. I work with many people and rarely meet anyone who fully understands all of their own strengths, weaknesses, habits, needs, drivers, desires, motivations and values or their personality traits, feelings, emotions, biases, patterns of behaviour and thinking.

Some people have no desire to acknowledge, let alone understand, why they become angry, jealous, impatient, or are scared to speak up and this failing to understand what makes you tick is dangerous. If you don't understand yourself, you risk misjudging other people, jumping to the wrong conclusions, being too harsh about others' weaknesses. If you think you're perfect, you're likely to blame other people when things don't work out as planned. Acting like this will make you an appalling leader.

Face your blind spots, no matter how dark

No one's asking you to share all of your weaknesses and bad habits openly. Just be honest with yourself and acknowledge your own mix of useful and unhelpful patterns and behaviours.

The first step to doing this is to observe yourself with an open mind. Try keeping a written journal, and go online and take one of the many free personality tests that are available such as MBTI and DISC. Another way is to ask your friends, family and close colleagues. Explain to them that you want to improve yourself and that they can help you understand some of your strengths and weaknesses. It's important that they're honest with their answers, so make sure that they know you want the truth, even if they fear it may upset you. If you're not sure what questions to ask, pick some from the list below. Ask yourself these questions too and note your answers in your journal. Compare your responses to those of your colleagues, family and friends.

- When I fail to get my way, how do I respond?
- What seems to make me angry, moody or act negative?
- When stressed or upset, how do I tend to act and behave?
- What makes me jealous and envious, and how do I show it?
- How do I treat other people when I am in a good mood, and when in a bad mood?
- What do you most love and admire about me?
- What most annoys you about the way I am?
- What one habit or behaviour should I change to become a better person?

DISCOVER THE ART OF SELF-LEADERSHIP

'To successfully lead others, first get your own house in order.'

The hardest person in the world you'll ever have to lead and manage is yourself. Washing the dishes every day is the perfect analogy for what it means to lead yourself well. It's not hard to do, but do you get it done or do you just leave it for someone else?

As a leader, it can be easier to instruct other people to do the things you don't want to do. When you're dealing with other people you can employ all sorts of leadership styles and tools, from motivating and encouraging, through to forcing and threatening. When it's just you, all you've got is the self-talk in your own head, and your success depends on your willpower, drive and self-commitment. If you've set your alarm to get an early start on a busy day, do you spring out of bed as planned, or do you just hit snooze on repeat?

Self-leadership is the first level of leadership, and if you struggle to lead yourself it doesn't bode well for your ability to perform well at the other types of leadership shown below. You'll never successfully and consistently lead other people, lead leaders or lead an entire organization when you can't even lead yourself. That's why now is the time to get your own house in order.

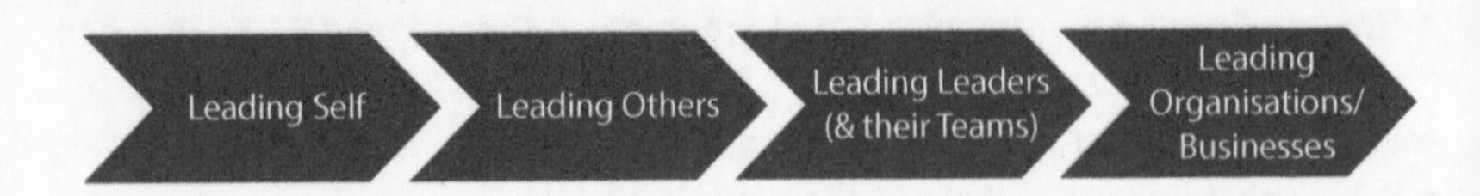

Make a self-leadership plan

Self-leadership involves managing how you act, behave, communicate and use your time. It covers every aspect of how you speak to, instruct, criticize and work with yourself. As a minimum, you need to:

- Make sure that you remember any goals and to do lists you set for yourself, and that you work towards achieving what you say you'll do.
- Maintain your healthy and good habits, while working to eliminate any unhealthy ones.
- Motivate yourself by trying to do things you enjoy that you'll find fulfilment in completing.
- Learn to say 'no', when needed, to requests from other people.
- Control your own emotions and how you communicate with other people.
- Be consistent in how you lead yourself and in how you lead others. As an example, if you want your team to be more creative, open-minded or punctual, you must also exhibit these same qualities.
- Be kind, compassionate and positive to yourself. You'll always have days when you make mistakes, forget to complete a task or say the wrong thing, and when this happens don't be over-critical and beat yourself up.

Find someone who will hold you accountable for working on and improving your own self-leadership abilities. Share with a close friend or trusted colleague your goals and actions for how you want to improve and ask them to observe, encourage and challenge you to stick to your plan.

DON'T WAIT FOR THE JOB TITLE

'True leadership doesn't start with a nice job title, corner office, company car or exclusive club membership.'

If you only start being a leader when you're given a leadership job title, you'll have waited too long and missed a golden opportunity to develop and practice your skills earlier on in your life and career. The sooner you can start practising, the sooner you can master being a leader.

In the many job roles and positions you hold before becoming a formal manager, you'll have plenty of opportunities to exhibit leadership. These come in all shapes and sizes and can be found in your home, school, college and community, as well as at your workplace. Leadership happens when you:

- Tackle an issue that others in your family are avoiding
- Organize client meetings when your boss is on holiday
- Take an informal lead on a project team when there's no appointed leader
- Make all the arrangements for your next family vacation
- Organize a sports tournament for university clubs and societies.

These are just a selection of ways you might lead without having formal authority, and all will give you hands-on leadership experiences. Informal leadership can even be practised with smaller tasks, such as organising a financial collection for a colleague or booking a team night out to unwind after completing a stressful project.

Successful leaders know that practice really does make perfect and that the practice should start as early as possible through informal leadership opportunities. Without doubt, this will lead eventually towards an official supervisory or management position.

Overcome your reluctance to lead informally

Always step forward when the opportunity to lead presents itself and you know it's appropriate for you. Being nervous and reluctant is understandable and common – your mind will be rehearsing any number of possible reasons why it's best not to step up. Classic examples include:

- Thinking you'll be told off or ridiculed
- Feeling it's not your responsibility or place to act
- Sensing you're not capable and will fail
- Being concerned about seeming too keen or visible
- Fearing that your boss or senior colleague will be offended
- Worrying that your colleagues may become envious and jealous.

Think objectively and honestly about any concerns you may have, by asking yourself if they're simply excuses because you feel uncomfortable about doing something for the first time or that seems out of character, or if the concern is valid and you're right to be cautious.

Informal leadership gets you noticed

Act at work as if you're in a leadership assessment centre, where potential new hires or high potential staff are tested and assessed for their leadership potential and given exercises in which observers look at who takes an informal lead when no formal leadership roles are handed out. The most impressive individuals are those who understand the situation they're in and take an appropriate lead of the activity, discussion, project or task. These people will receive the highest scores and be more likely to be hired or promoted. That's exactly how you must act in your workplace. As well as getting you noticed and giving you leadership practice, it will help you decide if you actually want a formal leadership role in the future.

USE YOUR INFLUENCE, NOT AUTHORITY

'You know when you've influenced someone well – it's when they convince others to follow your lead.'

Which is most important, influence or authority? Inexperienced leaders often think that being a leader means that you no longer need to exert influence because you can get your way by using authority. That's dangerous for two reasons:

- Your own staff might appear to accept your demands but if they're not happy and inspired, they're unlikely to be truly motivated and engaged.
- You're likely to be working alongside other leaders with teams of their own that you have no authority over. You can't simply instruct and order people who don't report directly to you – they don't have to listen to you, no matter how senior your job title.

Your typical working day will be filled with the constant need to influence and win people over, to get their agreement, buy-in or alignment on things that are important to you. Using authority is never the way to get people to:

- Accept your plans, goals, points of view, ideas or opinions
- Follow your vision
- Say, do or act in a certain way.

Successful leaders understand this and never rely on their job title to force their view. They understand that they have to convince and persuade through influence, to encourage people to positively carry out their requests and to believe in their ideas and directions. Quiet influence, not authority, is how to win people over to your way of thinking.

Put it into action

5

There are a few key skills needed to master the art of influencing:

- **Openly communicate**

If you want someone to do something they may not be keen on, don't simply email them – speak to them. Explain the importance of the work and why they're being asked to do it – and acknowledge the downsides of the task.

- **Be genuinely inspiring and visionary**

When asking someone to do something, it helps to show the impact of the requested task and how it fits into the bigger picture, overall plan or vision. By doing so, you'll more successfully inspire and motivate them.

- **Be likable and empathic**

It's human nature for a person to be more easily persuaded by someone they like and admire and is kind and nice. Become such a person by showing that you care by trying to understand the other person, for example, by understanding how busy they may be or why they may be reluctant to accept a task.

- **Leading by example**

It's very hard to convince someone to do, say or think something when you might be doing the opposite. The natural reaction in that situation is to think, 'Why should I listen to you'. The ideal is always to role-model and emulate what you're asking other people to do.

- **Giving and taking**

Reciprocity is key to successful interactions. Always try to offer something in return when asking someone to do something for you. For example, if you're asking them to work over the weekend on an urgent client project, offer them a day off in lieu.

- **Providing tools and support**

People will more readily be persuaded to do something when they have the necessary help and support from you. Always ensure that they have the necessary tools and resources to complete the tasks assigned to them.

BE VISIONARY WITH PURPOSE

'We are inspired to follow leaders who have found their true north.'

Which leaders do you most admire? No matter whether it's your current or ex-boss, or a globally recognized figure like Barack Obama, Richard Branson or Mark Zuckerberg, chances are you're impressed by the clarity of where they're heading and with what they aspire to create. It's their vision and sense of purpose that attracts you to them.

Individuals rarely write down their vision or purpose, but organizations do it all the time in the form of vision statements. You might have read some:

- Oxfam: 'A just world without poverty.'
- Amazon: 'Our vision is to be earth's most customer-centric company; to build a place where people can come to find and discover anything they might want to buy online.'
- Ikea: 'To create a better every day life for the many people.'
- Google: 'To organize the world's information and make it universally accessible and useful.'
- TED: 'Spread ideas.'

Leadership teams create these statements to outline where that organization is heading and what they want to become. They're normally a mix of big dreams, audacious goals, aspirations and values.

Successful leaders know that without clear goals you might go around in circles being pulled in different directions which can be both demotivating and energy-sapping. To avoid this, they work with their team to develop a vision statement to give themselves a clear understanding of where they're heading and of what they want to achieve.

By creating a vision statement, you'll stand out because very few leaders give their teams such clarity. A 2018 Gallup survey in the US found that only 22 per cent of employees surveyed strongly agreed with the statement that their bosses had any kind of clear direction, suggesting that four-fifths of all bosses have no idea where they're heading, or at least never think to tell their staff.

Create your own compelling vision

Create a vision statement as if it were the opening lines of a job advert for a vacancy in your team. It should clearly explain the team's focus and what it's aiming to achieve, and it should describe what people can expect when joining your team. The wording should be compelling and exciting enough to motivate and attract people to want to work with you and never want to leave!

To help you draft the ideal wording, take a blank piece of paper and write down your thoughts:

- Outline the vision of what you want to create and achieve with your team (over the next three, five or 10 years).
- Explain how you would like the team members to be led by you, work with you and also with each other to ensure that your vision will be realized.

Keep it simple

Summarize your wording into a key phrase or slogan which you can use to sell and get buy in to your overall vision. As an example, Boris Johnson and team did this to great effect by creating the line 'Get Brexit Done' during the UK's 2019 General Election. Share your overall vision with your team, asking them for their opinions and suggested edits so that you can create a final version which you're all willing to sign up to and work towards achieving. To serve as an inspirational reminder, create wallet-sized cards with the vision statement printed on and give each of your staff a copy for them to carry around or place at their workstation. You might also create vision posters which you can place throughout your office.

WALK THE TALK

'Make sure everything you do is aligned. Don't think one thing, say another, while doing something else entirely.'

You'll quickly have no one to lead if you ask your team to act in one way while you do the opposite. It doesn't matter if it's intentional or accidental, behaving like this destroys your credibility and the trust people have in you. No one likes working with a boss who:

- Encourages staff to be open and share, while regularly withholding information
- Insists that colleagues be on time for meetings, while always being late
- Persuades team members to support a company-wide initiative, while quietly undermining it
- Becomes angry when direct reports don't check their work for errors, while putting out mistakes themselves
- Comes down hard on someone for cheating on their travel expenses, while padding out expense claims.

If it's not obvious that this is unacceptable, ask yourself how you'd feel working with someone who acted like this. No one likes a hypocrite and although some of these might seem like minor flaws, they're often an indicator that the leader is unethical and acting without integrity in more serious ways in other areas of their work.

Successful leaders always walk the talk, aligning what they preach with their own choices, behaviours and actions.

Become a trusted role model

Start consciously role modelling the ideal behaviours and standards of excellence you'd like your team to adopt. This has to be done through leading by example, by personally demonstrating what you expect of others through your own words and actions. If you need people to be persistent, more strategic or less risk averse, then start acting in these ways. Even if it's not easy for you, show that you're trying and this will encourage and motivate your team to try to emulate you.

Be honest when not walking your talk

There may be occasions when you have to ask other people to act in ways that are different to what you do. When that happens, be honest about it. Think through how your team will react when they realize what's happening and explain the reasons for the situation. You may not be a details person, but need your team to become more details-oriented. Tell them what you need of them and admit that you struggle to concentrate on the small print. By admitting a weakness, you show vulnerability and the likelihood is that the team will respond by supporting you and the business goal, which remain aligned because of your openness.

SUCCEED FROM DAY ONE

'Get the beginning right – set the stage for what's to come.'

Your first few days and weeks in a new leadership role, particularly in a new organization, are critical. They will determine how successful you'll be in:

- Working with your new colleagues and team members. How you act and perform in this initial stage shapes how your working relationships form and develop. First impressions do count and how you're seen to be settling into your new role influences other people's perceptions and expectations of you.
- Achieving your goals and targets. The insights and knowledge you gain early on will determine how well you get a handle on your role and what it involves. Getting it right enables you to do the right things well.

Successfully transitioning into any new leadership role involves being thoughtful and not jumping into any new tasks and interactions without due care and attention. If you do, you risk making simple mistakes, underperforming and even falling out with people. At first, just:

- Listen: don't speak too much or share lots of opinions about how things could be improved and how they were better in your last company.
- Give people a chance: don't rush to make judgements on an individual's performance without fully appreciating all the context and recent history.
- Adjust to fit: observe the norms of your new organization's working culture and alter your behaviour accordingly.
- Soak it up: you don't need to create an instant impression by agreeing with everyone and saying 'yes' every time you're asked to do something. Take time to appreciate the intricacies of the issues, of your role and of what you're actually agreeing to.

Successful leaders know the importance of pausing and reflecting to minimize misunderstandings about what is happening around them.

Take a structured approach to onboarding

Onboarding, or the process of starting in a new role in a new organization, should be treated like a complex project that requires your full attention and careful planning. Put aside all your past experiences and assumptions and be open-minded enough to recognize that you don't know everything on day one.

Calmly listen to, observe and learn from your new colleagues and team members, appreciating how their behaviours, mindset and ways of working are different to your previous colleagues, and be open to doing things differently to how you have in the past.

Keep a journal of your notes and observations to help you record and reflect on any differences and similarities you observe (compared to your last role), especially around how:

- Colleagues communicate together and share opinions and ideas
- Colleagues thank and criticize each other
- Conflict arises and is dealt with
- Workspaces and offices are used and what is visible
- Goals, key performance indicators and other tasks are shared, delegated and achieved
- Colleagues motivate, inspire, support and challenge each other
- Colleagues request help and resources
- Budgets, forecasts and plans are created, agreed upon, implemented and monitored
- Good and poor behaviour and performance is recognized, rewarded and dealt with
- New colleagues such as yourself are acknowledged, welcomed and helped to succeed.

IT'S NOT A POPULARITY CONTEST

'If you want to be the most popular person in the room, sign up for a beauty pageant.'

As a leader you have to be ready to communicate all kinds of difficult messages, often in the space of one day. Leadership is definitely not a popularity contest. You need a thick skin to make the tough calls, which sometimes may appear very ruthless and out of character:

- Informing an eager team member that they're not being considered for a promotion
- Sharing with your team that they've not won a new high-profile project they wanted to work on
- Informing a colleague that a candidate they're keen to hire into their team didn't impress you when you interviewed her
- Expressing your frustrations at your team's lack of progress
- Denying a colleague their request for holiday leave because too many other colleagues in the same team will be out of the office in that same period
- Telling a team member that they will be fired if they do not immediately stop speaking badly about your strategic plan
- Giving a colleague an ultimatum to either accept and flow with your vision for the company, or to resign.

Of course, you'll get your share of positive news to share too, but it's the way you handle the bad that defines your leadership ability. Successful leaders know that difficult messages have to be communicated without any delay. To do anything else is to give people the wrong picture, false hope and incorrect expectations that will have a negative impact on motivation and productivity. When you have bad news, communicate your message as professionally as possible and be ready to manage the reactions of those you're speaking to, who may be shocked, upset, sad, confused or even angry. Very few leaders do this well.

Don't put off what you can do today

Never avoid sharing negative messages for fear of causing upset or to avoid being unpopular and getting into a confrontation. There's nothing to be gained from putting off sharing bad news, delaying a feedback session or sending a challenging email. You're not doing anybody any favours by delaying, and the sooner people know the hard truth the sooner they can start processing it, dealing with their reactions and, hopefully, planning how they learn, adapt and positively move on.

Plan communication well

Good news is easy, but when you're giving someone bad news or critical feedback it's especially important to plan your message well. Take your time to plan out the conversation or draft the email. Pause and reflect once you've prepared everything and re-read your draft or ask a trusted colleague to sense-check your communication plan.

The secret is to have a clearly stated and to-the-point message which is not too harsh and undiplomatic. No matter whether you're turning down a request or giving a colleague constructive feedback, always aim to clearly explain the facts, along with your observations and opinions.

Whenever possible, try to give the message in person and in private. If you can't meet them in person try meeting by video conference, so that you can see each other. It's best that emails, letters and phones are only used as follow-up communications.

Have a thick skin

Don't take the reaction to bad news personally, no matter how angry or upset the other person becomes. Show empathy and sympathy, telling them that it's okay to be upset or confused. Give them time to process what you have told them.

LISTEN WELL

'Switch off all those distractions swirling around your head and really listen – and think about what you want to say.'

It's really obvious when someone's not listening to you. You may not quite know *how* you know, unless they're looking at their phone while you're speaking or talking over you, but you'll know. These are the tell-tale signs:

- They never clarify anything you've said
- They don't ask any follow-up questions
- They cut you off or change the subject.

It's frustrating when it happens and it's normal to find this kind of behaviour demotivating and demoralizing as we all value being heard and we appreciate other people listening to what we are trying to say.

Successful leaders know that listening well helps people feel and perform better. This is borne out in a study of leaders' listening skills involving 3,492 managers, summarized in the Harvard Business Review. It found that the top five per cent of leaders in terms of listening skills stood out through:

- Creating conversations that were healthy two-way discussions involving helpful questioning, with little defensiveness shown when their comments and ideas were challenged
- Leaving those they listened to feeling more positive and with higher self-esteem
- Making those being listened to more open to hearing suggestions in response to what they were saying.

Show that you're actively listening

Aim to always fall into the top five per cent for your listening skills. You can achieve this by doing the following when someone's talking to you:

- Stop everything else you're doing and give the person in front of you all of your attention. If you're unable to do this, plan another time when the two of you are both free to have the conversation.
- Talk together in a location that's calm and free of noise, distractions and interruptions, and put away your phones and computers.
- If you have limited time, say so, and set a duration for the discussion, offering to continue the conversation later as needed.
- Demonstrate that you're present and listening:
  - Look at the other person and use engaged body language such as nodding, smiling and maintaining eye contact.
  - Say things that demonstrate you're really present such as 'I hear you', 'Sounds challenging' or 'Mmmm not easy'.
  - Summarize or paraphrase what you've heard, and if necessary ask questions to clarify your understanding.

Do people want to talk to you?

Having good listening skills isn't enough. You need to be approachable too so that people actually want to open up to you. Make sure that you're someone people are happy to talk to by eliminating distancing habits and behaviours, such as leaving your door closed, always acting busy, cutting people off mid-sentence, ignoring what they're saying or jumping to conclusions before they've finished speaking. If you're not sure how good a listener you are, just ask your team.

DEMAND EXCELLENCE

'Leadership is all about doing the right things and doing them right.'

You must make sure that your team or organization is doing the right tasks, and that those tasks are all being done really well. This is a hard balance to achieve. The awful truth is that most leaders and their teams do some important tasks badly, while also focusing on completing unimportant or unnecessary tasks.

I compare this to the simple metaphor of digging a hole in the ground. There's no point in digging a hole really well if it's in the wrong place; or, of course, digging a poor-quality hole in the perfect location. In the workplace, these two types of mistakes are far too common. For example:

- A team member spends hours creating a perfectly crafted spreadsheet or written report, only to discover that he had misunderstood the question or problem to be solved.
- You present a solution to a client in a very professional manner, only to hear that the client had asked for information about a totally different product.
- A key member of your team is given a great opportunity to present work to your global management team, but prepares badly and performs worse.

You'll never achieve excellent results if you or your team misplace and waste your energy, focus, time and resources in this way on the wrong tasks and/or complete essential tasks in a shoddy and poor-quality manner.

Challenge and support your team to achieve excellence

Excellence is doing the right things well all the time. To achieve this, make sure that each of your team has the right guidance and tools in each of six areas (collectively known as *Gilbert's Six Boxes*):

1. **The right information and feedback to know what to do.** Give them written job roles and responsibilities, guidelines explaining what needs to be done and why. They also need sufficient informal and formal feedback.
2. **The right tools and resources to do their work optimally.** Sometimes it's as simple as giving someone a new and faster computer.
3. **The ideal incentives to exceed expectations.** Give clear rewards for high performance, for achieving the goals and key performance indicators (KPIs).
4. **The ideal skills and knowledge to enable them to excel.** It's not enough to send someone on a training course or to give them the work experience – make sure they know how to use what they have learnt.
5. **The capacity to do what is asked of them.** Are some of your team out of their depth and struggling with the range of tasks/volume of work given to them?
6. **The motivation and commitment to work hard.** Do they like coming to work for you, enjoy completing their tasks and working with their colleagues?

HOLD FIRM TO WHAT YOU BELIEVE

'It's not easy to stay still while buffeted by the winds of peer pressure, group opinion and the views of the majority.'

There are times when being a leader will leave you feeling pressured, particularly when you're standing still or moving in another direction while everybody passes you, urging you to follow them. But you may do so because you know that your opinions, views and convictions are right and theirs are not. Having your own opinions and views and sticking to them is not easy but you have to sometimes if you wish to be successful.

Your opinions, views and convictions come from your life experiences, knowledge and long-held beliefs:

- Some are based around your mindset and behaviours, for example: hard work must be rewarded, you only get one chance, integrity is non-negotiable...
- Others are goal and target specific: we must enter into this new marketplace, our system has to be updated for us to succeed, that business has to be more profitable or we close it down...
- Others may focus on how things are done: we must always plan quickly, must collaborate in a certain way...
- Occasionally they may be more holistic and long term: a strong belief that our products must change the world for the better, all our decisions have to be sustainable in terms of their environmental impact...

Every leader has a mix of opinions and convictions. The most successful leaders always seem to know when to hold firm to what they understand or believe in, even when the tide of opinion moves in the opposite direction or their colleagues' views and direction is different.

Strike the right balance ... sometimes you're right and must hold firm

You must decide yourself when to hold firm to what you believe in, when others beg you to do the opposite. To help you achieve this:

- Listen and reflect upon the opinions and convictions held by your colleagues and try to understand where they're coming from.
- Analyse and reflect upon your own thinking and have an open mind about whether it's right to hold onto your opposing views.
- When you decide that you need to hold firm, prepare to explain your feelings, logic and reasoning. This can help justify your own views and increase your chances of winning others over to your thinking.

Some people may struggle to understand and accept your views, particularly when they are diametrically opposed to their own beliefs and thinking. They may get upset with you – try to accept this and not allow it to negatively impact your working relationships. Over time, people may come to recognize that you were right to hold firm.

... and sometimes you may be wrong

Remember: nothing is permanent – your convictions evolve and change as you gain more insight, information, experience and wisdom. You may have moments when you realize that a particular belief or assumption you held strongly is wrong and what you thought to be true is no longer the case. Admit it with humility to colleagues and openly embrace your new thinking, belief or view.

MASTER OFFICE POLITICS

'Being a leader is like playing snakes and ladders – never knowing when you will fall down the snake or rise up a ladder.'

Nearly every leader I have coached has spoken about their struggles with different kinds of internal politics and of needing to survive when colleagues play games with each other. One leader recently spoke of feeling worn out trying to survive internal political struggles within her company, describing her work environment as a jungle, where colleagues would do whatever it took to gain resources and recognition, some colleagues no longer on speaking terms and some having already resigned. Perhaps you have experienced internal politics yourself, such as:

- Your reputation being muddied by colleagues gossiping about errors of judgement you're accused of making
- A colleague choosing to not warn you about serious problems with a project you're leading
- Another department passing the buck, claiming to bosses that it's your team at fault, when you know this is not true
- Before a budget planning discussion, discovering that colleagues have been sneakily making arguments to the head of finance behind your back about why their departments and not yours deserve extra headcount next year
- Another business unit transferring a team member to your area with glowing references, neglecting to say that she was a poor team player
- Realizing that your boss is showing extreme favouritism to certain colleagues, which is negatively impacting upon you and your team.

To be a successful leader, you need to become used to such scenarios. Build up the experience and sense to know when and how to speak up and challenge, and when to keep quiet to avoid making a fraught situation worse.

Be a master navigator

Navigating your way through internal politics is not easy. You'll need all of your soft skills, in particular being able to influence, speak up, face conflict, communicate clearly, give clear feedback and be assertive. In addition:

- Never immediately jump up and down and assume the worst. When a colleague does not tell you something important, you might be tempted to angrily speak up assuming that their silence was deliberate and intended to put you in bad light. Don't do it! Perhaps they had simply forgotten. Instead, calmly explore and check what is actually happening and what people's real intentions are.
- Choose your battles – learn to work out when to let go of something, to not speak up, defend, justify or complain. Think carefully before doing the opposite and getting involved in an attempt to right a wrong, stop an inappropriate behaviour or set the record straight, perhaps to clear your name or show that your team is performing a task well when accused of the opposite.
- Keep your ears open and use your intuition to sense when an issue with a colleague might be brewing. For example, they may be starting to treat you differently to normal and now seem to avoid you or hold back from sharing ideas with you. Don't react negatively, do the opposite and spend more time connecting with and befriending this colleague – you may be able to warm up the relationship rather than leaving it to go cold.
- Maintain a healthy and positive relationship with your own boss. You need them on your side because they can serve as your biggest supporter or defender, helping you clarify or quash any rumours that might circulate about you or your team as well as stamping out other types of internal politics that you may face.
- Don't create any internal politics yourself – never spread bad gossip, innuendo or half-truths about other people. If you can't speak highly about other people, just say nothing.

THINK ABOUT CONTEXT

'I love the idea of "horses for courses", which means carefully choosing the horse you will ride for each race based upon the racetrack conditions.'

Far too many leaders treat every similar-looking situation exactly the same, failing to recognize that each may demand a different type of response to ensure the ideal outcome.

In your home, do you have a toolkit filled with various tools and you choose the best tool to solve each particular issue – perhaps a small screwdriver for one job and a drill for another? You'd never try to solve all your repairs and maintenance with the same tool, would you? The same applies to leadership – don't use the same leadership style in all scenarios. Surprisingly, many leaders ignore this basic truth and never vary how they act and respond even in markedly different situations:

- Dealing with every employee performance issue identically
- Motivating all team members with the same incentives
- Always communicating information via the same type of long emails
- Reacting in the same manner to staff struggling to meet deadlines
- Chairing all meetings in exactly the same style
- Using the same clichés and comments to express their feelings
- Asking the same tired old interview questions, no matter what level of role they're interviewing for.

Treating each person or problem in the same way is inefficient and rarely 100 per cent effective. People may become confused or lost, follow your incorrect advice and struggle, or feel misunderstood and become demotivated. This is not what you intended or in your best interest...

Learn to mix and match

Aim to become a situational leader, a leadership style made famous by Ken Blanchard, in which you need to recognise each unique situation that you're facing and respond in the most appropriate way by:

- **Always taking time to understand the issue.** Calmly assess what is happening before you respond. Explore and understand the full context of the issue or problem facing you, including whether it's a recurring issue. Also determine who is involved, noting whether they're experienced, newly hired, overworked or demotivated and so on.
- **Defining the optimal outcome.** Once you grasp the uniqueness of each situation facing you, you can then determine what the ideal outcome or solution you need to achieve is.
- **... and finally, deciding how you achieve your outcome.** Decide what the unique combination of ways you need to act and respond is in each case:
  - Sometimes you need to calmly listen and motivate and at other times act quickly to show your team your upset or concern.
  - In some situations, you need to act inspirational and visionary and in others to become involved in the details and micro-manage.
  - The list of possible ways of responding to different situations is endless. You can choose to sit down one-on-one and coach someone, lead a brainstorming discussion, ask how you can help, pause and act later, spend time observing or do absolutely nothing at all.

Only a lazy or inexperienced leader uses the same leadership tool every time.

GRASP THE BIGGER PICTURE

'Sometimes we become lost among the trees and are unable to see which way to move.'

Successful leaders understand the importance of taking a bigger-picture view. They step back from their day-to-day issues to do so. It's like being an airline pilot who is always breaking through the clouds to spend time higher up to see what is sometimes called a bird's eye or balcony view. This essential leadership task gives you space and time to:

- Better see patterns between issues, activities and problems
- Take a more strategic view of your responsibilities, challenges and goals
- Look ahead into the future rather than being caught up in the present
- Give your team the space to flourish, without you peering over their shoulders and constantly micro-managing them
- More time and insights to better plan how you can support your team and other colleagues.

Few leaders do this well – they get into the habit of being immersed in numerous daily issues, working through and ticking off tasks on to-do lists, dealing with urgent tasks like a firefighter and keeping a close eye on their team's work. Many leaders can't help doing this because in their more junior positions they were never expected or encouraged to take this balcony view. The risk is that your leadership performance will suffer if you don't regularly step back to take in the bigger picture. Only by stepping back can you truly appreciate why it's so valuable and important to do so.

Try zooming out

Think of yourself as a professional photographer. Zoom out to take great photos of entire landscapes and views of your working environment. As you rise into more senior leadership roles, this trick becomes even more essential. If you find it difficult to do, work out what is holding you back:

- During your working day, observe yourself to notice whether and when you spend too long involved in the details of your team's tasks and to-do lists. Ask yourself 'Is this really productive?'
- Overcome any barriers that stop you from stepping back. You may actually be more comfortable being in the details; you may not trust your team being left alone with day-to-day tasks; you may be nervous about stepping up into a new, more strategic and reflective role.

Make time to stand on the balcony

- Set aside time in your working week to be more strategic and bigger-picture focused. At these times, standing on the balcony above your work environment, reflect upon your medium- to longer-term workload and challenges as well as the more strategic issues and challenges facing you and your colleagues. What do you see?
- If this is difficult, have you thought of engaging with an executive coach or mentor to help you focus and reflect upon these longer-term and bigger-picture aspects of your work?
- It may also help you get used to taking a bigger-picture view to find opportunities to attend strategic and longer-term focused events and activities. You could try volunteering to sit on a restructuring or long-term planning committee, or attending conferences on future business trends or emerging business ideas.

YOU CAN'T RUSH BECOMING AN EXPERT

'Little by little, we grow in skills and expertise.'

You just can't become a leadership expert overnight. You can't short cut the process of acquiring various experiences and skills from which you learn and gain knowledge and wisdom. As a result, your own journey to leadership expertise will probably meander or hurtle down a familiar route, such as:

- You start out as a first-time manager with limited exposure to the rough and tumble of facing leadership responsibilities and situations. You may have attended Business School courses and other leadership skills training, but won't have had many years to implement and master your learning.
- Over time, you gain more leadership exposure and experiences, which when combined with mentoring, coaching and training enable you to start becoming and feeling like an experienced leader.
- Until, hey presto, one day you're viewed as an expert and are being asked to mentor others and to be a keynote conference speaker at company events, with people queuing up to hear you share your wisdom!

This journey to becoming an experienced leader takes time and patience. In today's culture of everything being on demand, this is not easy and we can easily forget that becoming expert at something takes time and that being able to quickly learn something does not make you an expert. Some young leaders mistakenly think merely having an MBA makes them skilled in leadership, ignorant that genuine expertise can only be gained through repeated real-life experiences. If you start prematurely thinking you're an expert, you risk becoming overconfident and likely to think you can take on more than you're capable of. This risks you making big mistakes that may even badly damage your career. Be careful.

Patiently follow a leadership development plan

Create your own leadership development plan and break down your annual goals and actions by month. This will encourage you to constantly:

- learn new things
- reflect upon your successes and struggles
- seek and act upon feedback
- ask others to mentor you.

Every leader needs a development plan, even if you are already running a successful business. Today's technology start-ups often have very young founders and CEOs. Their colleagues and shareholders understand the need to help these young leaders quickly build up expertise by helping them create leadership development plans. These might include providing the leaders with all kinds of tools and support, including having experienced and older mentors.

Be humble about how much you know

Always be open about the gaps in your own knowledge and experience. We all have such gaps. When facing different business and leadership challenges, recognize what is new to you and where you may lack experience or understanding. Don't worry about this – it's okay and expected that you be honest. Where you know you're not yet an expert, try responding to others by saying:

- 'Actually, I am not clear how to deal with this issue.'
- 'I am not sure. Who will have a better idea about what is going on?'
- 'I should know what to do but I am a bit confused. Let me reflect and sense-check with others.'
- 'How well am I understanding this problem?'

Being humble and honest in this way is an essential leadership strength, particularly when you're being promoted faster than you're able to gain expertise (which is becoming increasingly common).

LEADERS ARE SERVANTS

'It's their success, not yours that matters – nothing more and nothing less.'

Your role as a leader is to serve others in support of their own needs, aims and goals. It is not about focusing on your own successes and place in the history books. This concept of servant leadership may not be familiar to you but has been around a while and was first written about back in the 1970s by the American leadership expert and author, the late Robert K. Greenleaf.

The central point about being a servant leader is that you put your own success and needs to one side and focus on the needs and ambitions of your followers and other stakeholders. The benefits of doing so include:

- Colleagues working with and under you feel more valued, listened to and appreciated, and as a result will be more motivated, engaged and energized.
- Your customers and suppliers experience better interactions when working with your team members, which translates into more client loyalty and closer supplier relationships.

This selfless attitude of putting the needs and ambitions of others first can transform you both as a leader and a person:

- You become less competitive and stressed as you focus less on yourself and more on your team and colleagues.
- You keep your ego in check and stop needing to always come out on top, for example by winning arguments or dominating discussions in meetings.
- Consistently acting in this way enables you to become a true team player as you encourage your team members to contribute, be heard and to have the credit.
- You are more open and generous, for example willing to freely share ideas and let others run with them.

Little by little, become a servant

All leaders need to have their own needs, motivations and ambitions recognized and valued, and to seek job promotions, salary increases and bonuses. Nobody is suggesting that you stop doing this and become a pure servant leader. The secret is to continue being the way you are, but to make more space for the needs of other people by exhibiting a degree of selflessness.

When facing key choices and decisions, get into the habit of taking what I call the selfishness test by asking yourself, 'In this situation, whose needs am I primarily focusing on, my own or those of my team members and colleagues?' Review your answers to this question, and then decide whether you've got the balance right – sometimes your own needs come to the fore and at other times those of other people dominate. Hopefully, on many occasions, all of your needs will align.

Become more a 'we' and less an 'I' leader

When reviewing your work, don't ask yourself 'What have I achieved?' Think instead in a more collaborative fashion by asking, 'How have I helped my team, colleagues and/or organization to excel and prosper this week?' or 'Together, how are we excelling, growing and being motivated?'

Practise this way of thinking for a few months. You should find yourself becoming less of an 'I' person and spending more time in the 'we' space. Colleagues will hopefully notice this difference – ask them if this is the case. Hopefully, you'll receive some very positive feedback!

WATCH OUT FOR BIASED THINKING

'We rarely see the factual truths. Instead, we find ourselves staring at our own distorted image of the facts.'

The next time you make an important decision, do so at your peril. We live in an increasingly complex and volatile work environment where it's not easy to know what is actually happening. This is not helped by heavy workloads, including inboxes stuffed with emails and diaries crammed with meetings. How can you give sufficient time and focus to analysing, checking, reviewing data and information so you can arrive at accurate conclusions?

Even when we are sure that we've been thorough, we still risk making incorrect decisions and coming to the wrong conclusions. Here are some typical examples:

a. A new colleague acts very open and helpful during their first week of work in your office and you assume they will always be trustworthy.
b. You disagree with your company's decision to develop a new product and keep finding reasons to prove you're right, letting everyone know 'I told you so' when you find evidence to confirm your thinking.
c. Your team member is struggling to complete a piece of work and asserts that it's not their fault, and then blames other colleagues.
d. You're over-optimistic about the chances of your project team finishing their tasks on time, while another colleague thinks the opposite and is convinced that the team will always be late to finish such work.
e. Your boss has invested much time and energy into opening a new subsidiary and is now unable and unwilling to accept that it was a mistaken investment decision and that the new business should be closed down.
f. Your team are keen to implement a new system simply because they observe many other departments doing the same thing, even though they know that there are few business benefits.
g. You win a new large client with a proposal that contains new fee terms. Given this client win, you decide to always use this same winning fee proposal format in all future client bids.

Start understanding what is really happening

Learn from your mistakes. And don't stop there – learn from those made by others too. Start to understand the ways in which biased thinking may be clouding your judgement. Look again at the examples from the previous page. The following show the biased thinking in each example:

a. This is called the *halo effect* where we form a strong opinion based on a limited view. The danger comes from extrapolating and assuming that one good outcome means all future outcomes (with the same inputs) will be equally successful. We have forgotten how unique each situation might be.
b. This *confirmation bias* blinds us to the possibility that we are wrong. We are then unwilling to accept the possibility of having made a mistake and seek any possible justifications to prove we are right.
c. When we struggle to achieve a goal at work, we rarely blame ourselves and instead point our finger at others. This is known as the *self-serving bias* and can lead us to never learn from our own mistakes.
d. Such *optimism* or *pessimism biases* may cause us to see everything about a situation from either a positive or negative standpoint.
e. Called the *sunk-cost fallacy*, this is the tendency of not being willing to admit defeat after having invested so much time, credibility, money and/or energy.
f. Known as the *bandwagon effect* or *groupthink problem*, we can be taken in by ideas and opinions when many people around us hold them.
g. This type of thinking is called the *outcome bias* where we form a simplistic view of how we succeeded at doing something. Perhaps the fee proposal format was not very good at all and played no part in the winning tender.

The point to take away from all this is to step back, be open-minded, think of all aspects and angles and to question your own assumptions. Be okay about discovering that you or your team may have made a mistake.

PUT TRUST AT THE TOP OF YOUR LIST

'Trust is like a glue that holds everything and everybody together.'

Your number one role as a leader is to create and maintain optimal levels of trust. This is not easy because trust covers so many aspects of your work and interactions including:

- Trust in others, in what they're saying, promising, thinking and doing
- Trust in rules, laws, systems and procedures
- Trust in your own abilities, thinking and intentions.

When trust is missing or is being questioned, it's challenging to successfully lead because your colleagues might be distracted by their concerns, which may impact how they work in the following ways:

- I don't totally trust that I will be rewarded for performing well and exceeding my goals
- I hope I can trust my colleagues to help me when I struggle
- I'm not sure I trust that my boss has my back
- I never trusted the accuracy of the online invoicing system
- Be careful when working with that department, they can't be trusted to give us accurate data
- Although I went on the training, I don't trust myself with the new process
- I have little trust in the company's strategy and plans for new products.

It's normal to only think about trust when you suddenly realize that it's missing, for example when you lose trust in another person or no longer trust a process. It's also a very personal matter – something that you really trust might not be trusted at all by someone else.

Be a role model of trust

Your key trust-related task is to make sure that your colleagues trust you in all aspects of your work. They must trust that you can be relied upon 100 per cent in terms of what you say, promise and do.

Map out where trust is most needed

Try to understand how you can help raise the levels of trust:

- Between you and your colleagues
- Between your colleagues
- In the processes and systems your team works with, including those that you create.

Start by making a list of where trust is most needed. Base this on your own observations and opinions about where trust has been lacking and where it seems to be essential for creating the ideal work environment. Involve your team members by asking for their opinions. To encourage them to share more openly, create an anonymous online questionnaire for them to answer.

Proactively develop more trust

Once you know where trust is needed, explore how you can build it up in a sustainable manner. Trust is based on each person's perceptions and experiences, so it can be very hard to objectively pinpoint exactly what needs to be done. You may have to proceed by trial and error. Most of your actions will involve communication and sharing, for example:

- Make time for weekly one-on-one sessions between you and your team members to help build up their trust in you
- Have more team-building sessions and social gatherings between two departments to break down a lack of trust
- Hold discussions between your team and HR colleagues to share people's concerns about the accuracy of a new performance management system.

INTERVIEW LIKE A PROFESSIONAL

'If you want a high-performing team and organization, hire top performers.'

Far too many leaders moan about the quality of their team, despairing about their team members' poor motivation, mindset or willingness to adapt and change. Having to lead such a team can be very challenging and frustrating, particularly because it can stop you achieving high levels of success. A major reason for ending up with this problem is poor-quality hiring and you only have yourself to blame if you hire people who:

- Lack the ability to master the technical skills needed
- Fail to show any persistence and give up far too easily
- Always blame other people for their own problems and mistakes
- Show no interest in adapting to changes
- Show no desire to grow, take on more responsibilities and be promoted.

Sadly, most leaders invest too little time and effort into the recruiting process and may:

- Rely upon their HR colleagues and external recruitment companies to source and screen candidates, often never agreeing a clear job description or ideal candidate profile
- Never prepare for interviews with potential candidates, often not even reading their CVs
- Conduct interviews that are too short, where the leader speaks too much and simply asks random questions
- Leave HR to close the deal with a chosen candidate.

It's no surprise that many leaders become disappointed with their new hires and have to let them go and start the recruitment process all over again (which can demotivate their entire team and waste time and money). Successful leaders know that great hiring is the key to creating a high-performing team – any team is only as good as the people who join it. They also know that a poor-quality hire can't easily be transformed into a high-performing team member because there's only so much that interventions such as mentoring, coaching and on-the-job training can achieve to change a person's mindset and performance.

Be clear about what you're looking for

Decide what the critical success factors are for a person to succeed in a particular role. Make sure that these are clearly stated in any job advert and role description. Agree these factors with your HR colleagues and any external recruiters as the key criteria to use when approaching, filtering, selecting and shortlisting candidates.

Prepare well for interviews

Create a great set of interview questions to help you compare each candidate with the role's critical success factors. Develop so-called 'behavioural interview questions' to help you explore how a candidate has coped and dealt with particular challenges and issues. You could try:

- Tell me about a time when, working in a project team, you had to suddenly change direction and how you coped.
- Describe a situation when you made a big mistake and explain how you responded and what you learnt as a result.
- Give me examples that demonstrate how creative you are when faced with difficult goals and problems.

Catch candidates off guard

Most job seekers are well prepared and will have rehearsed their answers to questions they expect you will ask them. In order to learn about their real character and personality, you need to slip in a question or two that they won't be expecting.

Be just as thorough with internal hires

Before agreeing to take someone into your team or department, interview them as thoroughly as you would an external candidate.

KEEP UP IN A FAST-CHANGING WORLD

'Working life has become so volatile and uncertain – you could compare it to trying to remain seated while riding a rodeo bull.'

We live in a world of dramatic change and transformation, aptly referred to as the 'age of accelerations' by the *New York Times* columnist, Thomas L. Friedman. Industry disruptions, business revolutions and exponential changes are becoming commonplace, with leaders worrying about what will be the next Uber or Amazon business model that could suddenly appear and destroy their businesses. This speed of change is so dramatic that your leadership experiences and skills may quickly seem obsolete in the face of new challenges.

You need to expertly take your teams, stakeholders and organization forward in a so-called VUCA (volatile, uncertain, complex and ambiguous) world:

- The *volatility* is the result of events and situations changing faster than ever before, caused in part by new real-time processes and data processing.
- The *uncertainty* stems from this volatility with it becoming harder to know what is actually happening today or tomorrow.
- Thanks to technology, we have allowed everything to become more *complex* than in the past.
- All of this rapid change and complexity makes it harder to understand what is actually happening, with problems and solutions being less clear-cut and more *ambiguous.*

As a leader you're allowed to feel lost, confused and even stressed by all of this. But your challenge is to become a successful leader despite all this noise.

Turn VUCA to your advantage

To successfully navigate through your own VUCA business environment, follow this advice, which is expanded upon in later chapters:

Let go to make space for the new

What you thought or did yesterday might not be needed or even appropriate for the challenges facing you tomorrow. You have no choice but to be open-minded and humble enough to embrace the unknown, and be ready to learn, understand and adopt newly needed thinking and ideas.

Spend time in sense-making

Accept that events, problems and situations may not be as easy to understand as in the past. Together with your team, be ready to invest time in exploring and brainstorming sessions to help you all make better sense of everything.

Be comfortable when feeling unsure and lost

As a leader, you may feel that you should have all the answers and be certain of everything. Unfortunately, it's no longer possible to give your teams or even yourself clear direction, comfort or certainty.

Have the courage to face unexpected challenges

No matter whether you're facing a small business issue or something as big as a new Uber entrant wiping out a taxi's monopoly, it's okay to feel uncertain and to struggle to know how best to respond. The key is to face each challenge as best you can rather than ignoring it and hoping the problem won't be major and will simply go away.

TRY AN EXECUTIVE COACH

'Being coached is rather like openly and confidentially talking to your bathroom mirror, which listens attentively and asks some really insightful questions.'

Being coached is all the rage. I don't know of any global and well-known leader who has never sought the help of an executive, leadership or career coach. These are not like sports coaches who shout instructions from the side lines of the pitch. They're experienced individuals who provide coaching that is a combination of being:

- a transformative process for personal and professional awareness, discovery and growth, and the expansion of possibilities. [definition from the International Association of Coaching]
- a professionally guided process that inspires clients to maximize their personal and professional potential. [definition from the European Mentoring & Coaching Council]

Such a coach confidentially helps a leader sense-check how they could deal with any number of challenges, whether these are people management problems or behavioural and mindset issues. You could ask a coach about anything at all that will help you be a successful leader, such as how to:

- Deal with your over-critical boss
- Succeed in your new and complex role
- Inspire your team
- Create more balance in your work and life
- Lead with more stature and gravitas
- Turn your vision into reality
- Manage some older and demotivated team members
- Become more assertive and extrovert.

The coach is not there to give you black-and-white answers, but to help you arrive at your own conclusions and plans, to help you see things in a clearer and new light.

Find a coach you're comfortable with

Your HR colleagues will normally find a coach for you, and your organization will fund the cost. Try to meet at least two possible coaches in what are referred to as chemistry meetings. During these initial meetings, you're able to assess how comfortable you feel with both coaches and how well you sense that they understand you and your challenges.

Allow yourself to find value in being coached

Only by experiencing coaching can you discover its benefits. Why not start with two to three coaching sessions spread over a few months, with each session typically lasting one to two hours and spaced out at one per month. During each session, leave your office and meet your coach in a quiet and relaxing location. Bring to the coaching sessions your bag of topics that you want to reflect upon with the hope of discovering the perfect way to respond, solve or succeed.

Be ready for a conversation which might feel alien – the coach will, in confidence, listen to you deeply, show empathy, ask you lots of questions and encourage you to share your feelings, dreams, fears, goals and concerns.

PROJECT PASSIONATE POSITIVITY

'We all prefer to work in the sunshine surrounded by sunflowers, rather than to toil under dark and cloudy skies.'

Successful leaders create and maintain very positive working environments because this positivity translates into improved profitability, customer satisfaction and employee engagement. Studies confirm this – one by the University of Michigan and published in the *Journal of Applied Behavioral Science* found that positive and virtuous leadership and team practices help an organization to excel for three reasons:

- The positive emotions in the office help people to work well and be more creative together.
- The higher levels of positivity serve as a vaccine against negativity, there's less stress and people more easily bounce back from any setbacks.
- Employees feel better in general, enabling them to be more loyal and willing to perform at their best.

I have spent enough time within many organizations to observe that such positivity is highly contagious within a team or an organization. When a leader exudes positivity, their team feel better and they start to smile and engage together more, becoming more interactive and collaborative.

If you're already positive, be a role model

Being positive might come naturally to you and you may always be cheerful, full of high energy and see the best in people and situations around you. If this is the case, then please continue being such a role model and share your infectious positivity, which others will emulate and copy.

If you're not positive, then change

Perhaps you struggle to be happy and positive all of the time? You're not alone. You may even feel that you a naturally negative person. It's not easy shedding a tendency towards a negative personality and I have known leaders who admit to being comfortable holding onto a negative and pessimistic mindset and having no desire to change it.

This may to some degree be due to where you're working, or have been working. You'll find it easier to break such a negative mindset or habit by trying to work in environments that are positive, forgiving, fun, caring and filled with laughter and happiness. Finding such an environment might mean having to resign from your job to move to a healthier working culture.

You might also seek help from a life coach or a therapist who specializes in cognitive behavioural therapy (CBT). Through a number of CBT sessions spread over at least a few months, you could radically change the way you think and behave regarding yourself, your work and life.

WHAT ARE YOU READY TO SACRIFICE?

'So often you must give up something such as time, options or energy in pursuit of your goals.'

Think about what you may be willing to give up in pursuit of creating a successful leadership career. It's impossible to achieve all of your leadership-related dreams and goals without sacrificing something. Examples of sacrifices that leaders have to make include:

- Time is the most common, given that you only have a finite number of hours in each day and you can't be in all places at once. Many leaders give up family time at evenings or weekends to make space for teleconferences, emailing, business travel and meetings, as well as dealing with ad hoc crises, emergencies and deadlines.
- Letting go of the past is also a common sacrifice. As an example, you might have been a successful salesperson used to closing your own client deals and earning large sales commissions. When promoted to lead a sales team, you may lose having your own sales wins and have to adjust to helping your sales team close their own deals.
- As a leader, you must sometimes sacrifice your own needs to put the needs of your team first in order to motivate and inspire them, which involves listening and responding to their needs. As a result, there will be times when their opinions, views and goals will overrule yours.
- One day, you may have to make the ultimate sacrifice – that of resigning and giving up your leadership role to take the ultimate responsibility and accountability for serious mistakes or poor performance by you or your team.

Sacrifice to set the right example

If you're a leader who makes sacrifices, this can be very inspiring and motivating to your team. It can make it easier for them to do the same.

- By working over the occasional weekend, you can encourage them to do the same thing when needed
- Putting your own needs aside in place of theirs may encourage them to do the same with other colleagues.

These are examples of you leading by example, which is an essential skill for any successful leader.

Are you comfortable with your sacrifices?

Try to think through your choices before you make them – you don't want to regret sacrifices later. As an example, there's little point in working long hours to gain a promotion at the expense of ruining your marriage and never seeing your kids before they go to sleep. You'll have achieved short-term career success at the expense of later looking back in anger at how foolish you've been.

Some things are not negotiable

Never sacrifice your ethics, integrity and character to simply help you achieve your leadership ambitions and goals. Examples might include not cheating by stealing ideas and claiming them as your own in order to further you career, or not pretending you have completed a task simply to earn a bonus.

DON'T SAY 'YES' IF YOU MEAN 'NO'

'We live in a world of falsehoods with people rarely saying what they really think.'

Stop replying 'no' when you really mean 'yes', and 'yes' when you really mean 'no'. Instead, start being honest and stop hiding what you feel, think and want. We all are guilty, to a greater or lesser degree, of doing this and sometimes for very good reasons, such as:

- To not upset or hurt someone else
- To enable someone else to win an argument
- To leave ourselves in our comfort zone.

As a leader, you must live to a higher standard than others do given that you have a responsibility to those following you. No matter whether you lead a small team or an entire global organization, you lead others and your words, actions and decisions can have a big impact on them. There are so many ways in which you and your team are impacted when you mix up saying 'yes' and 'no':

Agreeing and saying 'yes' when...	Saying 'no'...
• Requested to take on more work, even when there's no spare capacity within your team • Asked to shorten a project timeframe, leaving yourself with an impossible deadline to meet • Asked whether you agree with your boss's opinion on an important topic, even when you really don't agree • Told to accept some cuts to your department's budget and headcount, which you know are unreasonable and will make it impossible to meet next year's sales targets	• To a job promotion, because you're in your comfort zone and fear you won't succeed in the new role, even though you know it would be a great career move • To an opportunity for you and your team to present to your global board of directors, because you're uncomfortable making public presentations, even though the visibility would be fantastic for you and your team • To leading a project team, in spite of the great exposure and experience the role would give you

It's time to stop acting in this dishonest way and to come clean.

Do the right thing, starting today

When facing the dilemma of whether to say 'yes' or 'no', take time to think and reflect in order to determine when a *yes* is the ideal answer and when *no* is the optimal response. Once you have reached a decision, have...

...the courage to say 'yes'

- To seizing the opportunities you want, in spite of having anxieties and fears of entering into the unknown
- To leaving your comfort zone, in spite of the fear of taking on something new
- Even if it may shock or upset other people
- By speaking up and overcoming any shyness, modesty and introversion.

...the strength to push back and say 'no'

- No longer accepting feedback, requests and advice which you don't agree with
- Through being assertive and clear in your communications
- With a thick skin to help you face any criticism and peer pressure
- Accepting that you may upset your colleagues, particularly if you had always said 'yes' in the past.

These steps are not easy and sometimes you just have to make a start and jump in.

SEEK AND EMBRACE FEEDBACK

'Positive, constructive feedback to a leader is like water and sunlight to a plant – the energy enabling the leader to grow, expand and flourish.'

Imagine that you never ever received feedback, opinions or observations of any kind about your behaviours, styles, habits and work performance. You might feel you're perfect because no one ever commented about or criticized you. However, this would be dangerous because without any feedback you'd never know how you can improve and grow as a leader and whether what you're doing is perfect or a total disaster. You'd be blind to how others perceive and experience you. This would be like driving a car with no side- or rear-view mirrors, and everything around you as you drive would be blind spots you can't see.

Successful leaders always seek feedback to provide them with a clearer understanding of what other people think about and expect of them, their team and work. The insights gained help them improve how they lead themselves and others.

You don't have to agree with everything you hear, but isn't it better to know what others are thinking and feeling, rather than being left in the dark? Thankfully, feedback is normally free and easy to obtain and you can seek it about any aspect of yourself and your work, such as how well you're leading, motivating, communicating, making decisions and collaborating. You can seek feedback from anyone who knows you and your work, although not everyone you ask may be willing to respond to your request and you must respect their wishes. Some people may be reluctant to share anything negative for fear of upsetting you or they may feel they don't know you well enough or simply have nothing of value to share.

Proactively seek regular feedback

First of all, find out whether your organization already has a feedback gathering process in place. The most common kind is an annual or bi-annual 360-degree online survey in which the responses are collected together and given to you as anonymous feedback.

Such a formal process is a great start, but is nowhere near enough! It's better to also seek feedback on a more regular basis and in a more informal manner so you can gauge how you and your leadership work are seen. Ask those who report to you to give you monthly feedback in the form of answers to these questions, with their answers ideally being given to you verbally:

- 'What are your observations about me as your boss over the last month, and what did I do well and not so well?'
- 'During the next month, what would you recommend I focus on doing more of and/or doing better?'

This second question is known as feedforward as opposed feedback, and it's where you ask people to give you advice for the future rather than about your past behaviour.

Always thank those who give you feedback by dropping them an email or telling them in person. You are not expected to act upon every suggestion you may be given, but do take on board any suggestions and advice which could help you become a better leader.

DEAL WITH RESISTANCE TO CHANGE

'People rarely jump for joy at the sight of something changing in their lives.'

There's always something changing, something new or different occurring and it's rare for anything to stay the same for very long. For a leader, dealing with all the changes around them can be incredibly hard. A typical leader might be feeling comfortable and good about the way things are flowing and suddenly along comes a big scary change, causing them to feel:

- Confused, demotivated, upset, uncomfortable and even fearful
- Unwilling to accept the change, and instead choosing to resist and fight back
- So opposed that they may even choose to resign!

It's human to struggle in this way because it's hard to have to let go of the old to let in the new, to give up the familiar for something unknown. Such reactions to change are comparable to how you cope with the death of a loved one. In her famous work, Dr Elisabeth Kübler-Ross describes a predictable process of grieving, which is exactly the same process we go through when dealing with any challenging change. The stages of this process are:

- Being shocked and surprised
- Feeling anger, frustration and confusion
- Wanting to negotiate and bargain
- Finding acceptance.

Successful leaders become used to taking themselves and their teams through this process of dealing with change.

Work through the grieving process

Working alone or with your team, you need to work through the different stages in order to successfully confront, understand and accept any change.

- Allow time to get over any shock and surprise but don't deny the need for the change or ignore the fact that a change is really going to happen.
- Understand why there may be a need to change and seek to understand the positive reasons and benefits of the change. Share these with your team to help them view the changes in a more positive light. Sometimes this may be difficult if you or your team feel the change may be unnecessary and even a bad thing, and no amount of positive spin would alter this thinking.
- Allow your team to express their feelings and help them to understand that any change takes effort, can seem daunting and that it's common for someone to be anxious and even fearful when facing something new like this.
- Make time for people to discuss the change. It's natural for someone to want to know if the change has to happen now and as planned.
- Help and encourage your team to become comfortable, to accept rather than simply be resigned to living with the change. It obviously helps if you're also accepting and okay with the change and have already overcome any of your own concerns and reservations. So try to work on yourself first.

Allow some people extra time

Some people really struggle with change. Spend extra time talking with them to understand why they're resisting or unhappy about the change, and try very hard to respond to their concerns. For example, if they:

- Hold back because they lack the necessary new skills or knowledge, make sure they know that you can arrange training
- Worry they will struggle with new processes, offer to support them
- Feel burned out and view the change as the 'final straw', give them some time off or extra care and attention.

EMBRACE FAILURES

'To never fail is the easiest way of ensuring you're never successful.'

Do you worry about making mistakes, about making the wrong decisions and choices? You would not be alone if you do – nine out of ten leaders admit that the top concern keeping them up at night is a fear of failure. This finding comes from a 2018 survey by Norwest Venture Partners, who interviewed 200 CEOs and founders of privately held, venture- and growth equity-backed companies.

In our very uncertain world, failure is inevitable. You can minimize the possibility of it by employing all forms of expertise and wisdom to help ensure that your actions and decisions are perfect, but you'll still have days when for any number of possible reasons you might fail:

- Actual sales revenues are far below your sales forecasts
- The construction costs of a new factory are double the amount you budgeted
- The newly hired member of your team performs badly and must be fired
- Your negotiation strategy with a key supplier does not work
- You lose out to a competitor when trying to win a new key client account
- Your election strategy is weak and you come last in the vote.

How do you react when you don't achieve what you planned or when you have made a poor decision? Chances are you'll be embarrassed, worried for your job, wishing to hide the failure and perhaps deflecting the blame by pointing your finger at the person next to you. These are common reactions but, even worse, I have found that leaders sometimes put their fingers in their ears and actively avoid talking about their failures and act as if they never happened. Successful leaders, however, know that acting like this is a recipe for disaster. To improve as a leader, you must embrace your struggles and failures and explore the lessons they can teach you so that you grow, move on and never make the same mistakes again.

Have a mindset of experimentation

Be a leader who has a tolerance for failure and encourages their team to constantly experiment and explore, who tries out new ideas, new people and new ways of working and so on. Motivate and inspire your team to never hold back for fear of failing. Instead, encourage them to be innovative while understanding that things rarely go to plan and that sometimes an unsuccessful outcome might open the door to new successes and discoveries.

Learn from what's happened

Mistakes happen! It's your job as a leader to create a working culture where everybody understands this, and that you must all be open-minded and self-reflective enough to carry out a 'lessons learnt' exercise after each failure to maximize the return on the effort you've invested.

When failure does strike, sit down with your colleagues to openly explore and answer these two questions:

- 'What can we learn from this, what happened and why?'
- 'How can we grow stronger and wiser, to make sure we are more successful moving forward?'

Don't treat these sessions as opportunities to apportion blame and to hurt each other. They should be brainstorming sessions with the explicit aim of helping everyone to grow and become more successful in the future.

DON'T RELY UPON PAST VICTORIES

'Earlier career successes don't assure you of success today.'

The top-performing members of your team might be the worst candidates to lead the team for a number of reasons. Your worst mistake might be promoting them into a leadership position. For example:

- A top-performing salesperson who is 100 per cent focused on their own sales successes might struggle to step back and manage an entire sales team. They may be unwilling to give up their focus on their own work and find it hard to focus on training, encouraging and supporting the team in achieving their own sales and career goals.
- A dedicated software engineer is so used to working alone, relying upon their introvert personality to help them quietly think through problems, that they may struggle to lead a department that requires them to be an inspirational communicator.
- A workaholic and details-focused accountant is promoted into a Finance Manager role, and in their new role rarely delegates tasks. When they do they can't stop micro-managing their team members.
- The keenest and most dominant member of a marketing team is appointed its team leader. They are admired by senior colleagues but their immediate colleagues refuse to work under them claiming they are far too selfish, never listen and are only concerned with their own success and visibility.

It is common for someone to be promoted based on their past performance and in their new and more senior role they may struggle to be successful, perhaps unable to cope with the high workload or complexity of the problems. Sometimes referred to as 'being promoted to their level of incompetence', this is a common reason for someone who had been very successful to then unexpectedly fail in their career and even be fired. It's something that successful leaders never allow to happen to members of their team and also to themselves.

Differentiate between performance and potential

How do you separate a person's performance today and their potential to succeed in larger roles tomorrow? The same applies to you in terms of your own performance and potential. Most global companies recognize this and they monitor and reward their staff based on two separate criteria:

- Their actual work performance to date
- Their potential to grow in the organization and succeed in larger job roles.

For this reason, a high-performing leader or employee might earn large bonuses for exceeding their annual goals or key performance indicators (KPIs), yet may still not be viewed as ready for a promotion into a larger and more senior position.

Don't fail in your first leadership role

When you're fortunate enough to have been promoted into a leadership role, be humble enough to admit that the skills that got you this far may not be suitable or sufficient in your new role. To truly succeed in your new leadership position, you need some brand new skills, styles and behaviours. If you're not sure what are these are, ask your boss and those who may be in similar leadership roles to yours. Your new skills will probably include learning to:

- No longer do everything yourself and instead start delegating and empowering your team
- Stepping back rather than being details focused, micro-managing too much and not trusting other people's work
- Giving team members the credit rather than simply seeking it for yourself
- No longer being a sole contributor or loner, and instead needing to communicate more with others, moving from an 'I' to a 'we' mentality
- Keeping your emotions in check because now you have a team who will be influenced and impacted by your reactions.

LEARN, UNLEARN, RELEARN

'The best leaders are like school children – they spend their days learning.'

We live in a world where new knowledge and facts are appearing all the time. Until 1900, it was estimated that the amount of human knowledge was doubling every 100 years and, since then, this time frame has been dramatically shrinking. Today, it's estimated that total human information and knowledge is doubling almost daily. At the same time, a lot of knowledge is quickly becoming outdated and superseded – ideas that are valid today may have little relevance or value tomorrow.

As a leader, you must deal with this exponential growth of newly available knowledge that typically has a shortening lifespan of relevance and usefulness. We see this phenomenon everywhere:

- A new manufacturing or supply chain process becoming obsolete within a year
- Data on a new market for your products becoming useless in a few months' time
- Adopting new 'best practice' leadership styles and models being required on an almost annual basis
- Keeping up with never-ending new cyber-security threats and other risk management challenges
- Juggling numerous upgrades to every system and process you manage
- Continually adapting to new rules and procedures, on everything from data privacy to corporate governance
- Constant pressure to restructure and reorganize in the face of new evidence that things can be done better.

It's impossible to be a successful leader if you're not constantly learning, unlearning and relearning. Bad luck if you have no interest in reading articles or books, in attending conferences, or hearing about other people's ideas and experiences. You're doomed if you're uncomfortable in giving up your old opinions and understanding, to make space for new concepts and ideas. Leadership and learning are indispensable to each other. Very soon, CEOs may be known as CLOs (chief learning officers) and job interviews for management positions may focus on a candidate's willingness and ability to learn rather than on qualifications and achievements.

Adjust your mindset

Are you comfortable in having your assumptions, beliefs and understanding challenged by new ideas and accepting that much of your existing knowledge and understanding will become redundant? If not, you need to be!

Every month, carry out a knowledge audit by keeping a note of:

- The new ideas and concepts that you came across in the past month that seem important to your work but that you may not yet fully understand
- The relevant knowledge, processes, hard and soft skills that you need to start learning about
- Which of your old thinking patterns, ideas and knowledge are no longer relevant and have been superseded.

Find a like-minded colleague or mentor to discuss all of this with and to hold you accountable for pursuing any new learning and training, and to encourage you to let go of any out-of-date thinking and ideas.

Reading is key

There's always something that you can read or listen to which improves your knowledge and wisdom. It might relate to technical skills, leadership skills, to your organization or industry, or to the business environment.

Use your time wisely and always carry these reading materials with you to read in any quiet moments, perhaps when on flights or in taxis. You could also listen to podcasts as you drive to work.

PROACTIVELY SEEK OUT CHALLENGES

'You're not being a leader if you never step up to tackle issues and challenges.'

Leadership is an expedition – it involves taking teams, businesses and organizations forward into new and uncharted territory, where all kinds of challenges await. Such challenges may come from needing to embrace new opportunities, take full advantage of new ideas, technologies and markets, or from needing to cope with all kinds of problems, threats and risks.

All these challenges must be faced head on. Successful leaders will never avoid them no matter how complicated, unclear or downright dangerous they may appear at first glance. Sometimes they will be tackled with urgency and speed and at other times calmly only after careful planning. Great leaders often go one step further – rather than waiting for the challenges to arrive, they proactively hunt them out.

In addition to helping the organization, when a leader is willing to leave their comfort zone to pursue needed challenges, they also boost their own visibility and career opportunities. By putting up your hand and offering to take on challenges, such as leading difficult projects and tasks, you put yourself in the spotlight and senior colleagues may start viewing you as a 'go-to' leader willing to take on difficult, risky tasks that others are not.

Make challenge-seeking a habit

Get your team together and regularly brainstorm to uncover and assess all possible challenges that you may not yet have fully recognized and tackled. These challenges may already exist or they may be ones that you foresee arising in the near future. Such challenges may take all kinds of forms such as:

- You notice it's becoming harder to hire engineers
- Your plant is running out of an essential raw material
- A key client seems to be having worsening cashflow problems
- Key staff are retiring with no successors in place
- Tensions are rising between departments within your company
- A new competitor has just launched a lower-priced product that may take market share.

Be aware that your eagerness to take on challenging tasks may have its downsides such as needing to work longer hours and the risk of becoming stressed. Do be careful about going overboard on this one and seeking out problems to solve just for the sake of it and being viewed as someone who finds a challenge hiding behind every corner and lurking under every stone. Your team may become angry that you're creating more work for them unnecessarily.

Make a plan of action to tackle each challenge

You need to decide how to respond to each challenge that you discover and observe.

- Involve the relevant team members and colleagues to help you analyse and understand each issue and to decide how you'll tackle and solve it
- Decide whether the challenge needs to be responded to now, at a later date or can even be ignored altogether
- Create a plan of action
- Agree how you'll obtain the necessary resources and approvals to implement your plan of action.

EXPECT THE ODD STORM IN YOUR TEAM

'New team members can unsettle an existing team, like throwing a stone into a still pond.'

A team goes through a series of stages similar to those faced as we move from childhood, teenage years through to late adulthood. It's vitally important to help your team navigate the potentially disruptive early stages.

- **Forming stage**: This is the first stage when a team has just been created and everything is new, not fully understood nor aligned. Relationships are not developed, goals not aligned and tasks not agreed upon. An established team might fall back into this forming stage when there's a major change such as a new boss being appointed, new members joining or the goals and aims of the team being changed.
- **Storming stage**: You can compare this to a person's rebellious teenage years and is when team members become more settled and comfortable and start to learn what they can get away with. This might involve speaking up, challenging or cutting corners, and is a team's most difficult stage. If not managed well, this stage can result in conflicts, blame games and disruptive behaviour leading to poor relationships and weak performance.
- **Norming stage**: This is the time when a team is overcoming its storming stage challenges and is beginning to operate as an aligned and healthy team in terms of goals, trust and collaboration.
- **Performing stage**: This is the ideal stage of any team and is evidenced by high levels of motivation, interaction, accountability, responsibility, sharing – at this stage, any conflict tends to be healthy.

Do these stages feel familiar from teams you have worked within or led to date? They form part of a team development model, first proposed by a US professor of psychology, Bruce Tuckman, in the 1960s, which has stood the test of time and is a lens through which you can understand any team you're asked to lead. The model can help you focus on how you need to help your team to become a high-performing one as fast as possible.

Manage a new team well

- Pick new team members well in terms of personality, mindset and attitude to ensure that they will fit into your existing team. Always choose someone who is a team player over a very individualistic person when deciding who to hire or invite into your team, to make sure that the new person will collaborate and share with others.
- Introduce new goals, aims, processes and systems thoughtfully to minimize any misunderstandings, work overload, stress and demotivation. Spend extra time in communicating with all members so that they fully understand everything, including buy-in of any changes you need to make.
- As a new leader of a team, don't become the reason why your team's engagement and productivity might fall. Take things slowly and observe and listen before acting. Appreciate that your team will have been used to the style of your predecessor, and need time to adjust to your leadership style and expectations.

Overcome the storming stage

- What rules of conduct do you need to ensure that your team works smoothly and positively together? Create these rules and maintain them. They might include ideas such as if you need people to prepare well for management meetings, then say so and be consistent in demanding this. Likewise, if you need team members to quickly and positively help each other, make this a topic you regularly talk about and discuss.
- Spend time building up high levels of trust by encouraging open communication and addressing at an early stage any possible conflicts and misunderstandings.
- Invest in team-building activities and team social events to help speed up the bonding and trust-building process.
- Give each team member plenty of feedback in one-on-one sessions, and allow them to also give you feedback on your role as their boss. This open communication culture can allow people to share their concerns and worries before they become more serious issues.

PUT YOURSELF IN OTHER'S SHOES

'You will only truly understand other people when you try to see the world through their eyes.'

Showing empathy brings out the best in people. The people you show empathy to will usually feel valued and understood by you and appreciate that you're making the effort to understand their concerns, issues, needs and dreams. It's not only with your staff you can be empathic, but anyone you work with including colleagues, clients and suppliers.

- Having empathy for your clients allows you to fully understand the issues that they face and need your help in solving
- Similarly, by understanding your suppliers you're able to create a deeper and longer-lasting partnership of mutual understanding and aligned expectations.

Empathy is an awareness of other people – of their emotions, feelings, moods and needs. It forms part of emotional intelligence. Often referred to as EQ, your emotional intelligence comprises four key interlinking aspects:

- Self-awareness
- Self-management
- Empathy
- Social interaction.

Typically, if you have taken the time to know yourself well, to become self-aware, then you'll find it easier to be empathic. Being empathic is a choice and can be learnt and practised and is essential to any leader's success. Without it, you'll struggle to inspire and motivate your team and will be seen as a cold and uncaring leader.

Show empathy in challenging moments

If you wish to be recognized as a truly inspiring leader, make sure that you demonstrate empathy during difficult moments for your colleagues, organization or clients. Allow New Zealand's Prime Minister Jacinda Ardern to be your role model. In 2018, she showed immense empathy by spending time with grieving relatives of those killed in her country's mosque shootings. When a disaster or tragedy occurs, it can be so easy to focus on being jealous, angry or upset but it takes great leadership to also show compassion, understanding and caring.

At work, there are many examples of when your team will need your extra support and understanding:

- You lose a large client business and this deflates your sales team
- Your team becomes burnt out through overwork
- One of your team fails to complete a project on time and is very upset
- A key employee is poached by a competitor and the rest of the team must work overtime to fill her vacant shoes.

In such cases you must understand and acknowledge how your team is feeling, giving them time to talk, grieve, cry, take time out or de-stress.

Be tough with empathy

As a leader you'll always need to have difficult conversations and to give people critical feedback. Make sure, however, that you do it with empathy.

- When you need to tell somebody off, do so in private and keep your emotions in check. Talk to them calmly, giving them time to reflect and respond.
- If you need to terminate somebody's employment, do it but demonstrate your empathy by giving them as much notice, support and termination pay as possible.

KNOW WHEN TO SHUT UP

'So often, it's the words coming out of a leader's mouth that lead to their downfall.'

Are you the kind of leader who always finds something to say rather than stay silent? Too many leaders can seem desperate for others to hear their own voices, rarely keeping their own opinions and views to themselves. I am sure you'll have often noticed this habit:

- A person criticizing their colleague for being late for a meeting
- The manager who keeps making inappropriate jokes
- A leader always insisting on having the last word in any discussion, no matter how useful or inappropriate
- A team member always making comments about other people's appearance and lifestyle choices.

Acting in this way by always saying what comes in to your head is a recipe for disaster and will cause you to fail as a leader. Over time, you'll alienate more and more of your colleagues by not listening nor respecting them while appearing to belittle, over-criticize and demotivate them. As you become more senior, your words carry more impact and weight so can upset many more people. You can see this when observing global leaders, such as the US President or UK Prime Minister, whose messages can inspire or upset millions of people.

Be fast to praise, slow to blame

Before you speak, pause. Will what you're about to say make someone feel good and uplift them, or will it have the opposite effect of bringing them down and making them feel bad? Go ahead and share your positive words, but think before being negative and critical and decide whether it's absolutely necessary to upset someone with your words. Sometimes, you have to. But maybe you're being critical simply because you want to prove a point, win an argument or put someone in their place. You may simply be acting out of habit and, by pausing, you can decide whether you need to change what you plan to say. Try sleeping on it and, the following day, decide whether you still need to say what you had planned.

This same thinking applies to your jokes, off the cuff comments and stories. Some will leave a positive feel good feeling and are okay to share while others may be offensive, insensitive or discriminatory.

Pause before pressing 'send'

It's not just when speaking verbally that you should pause. You might be guilty of the same mistake in your emails. Emails are notoriously easy to without much thought. The next time you're about to press the 'send' button, pause and check the tone, meaning and intention of your message. Once someone else has heard or read your words, it's too late – you can desperately apologize but the damage is done. Try drafting your email and saving it as a draft. Come back to it later and only press 'send' if you're absolutely sure your choice of wording is appropriate.

PLAY TO YOUR STRENGTHS

'Focus on what's working rather than trying to repair what isn't.'

It's human to often look on the negative side in any situation before focusing on the positive. With people, we tend to always notice a person's weaknesses rather than their strengths. We do the same thing to ourselves, fretting about our faults rather than acknowledging and celebrating our positive qualities and strengths.

This spills over into the world of leadership development where we tend to focus on leaders' gaps and weaknesses. By doing so, we are trying to create great all-round leaders but this is a mistake. Using a sports analogy, how many sportspeople have been pushed to become all-rounders who excel across many sports? Very few, with the vast majority focusing on their areas of strength: David Beckham on his control of a football, Serena Williams on dominating a tennis court and Tiger Woods on his ability to precisely hit a golf ball. Imagine how much effort would have been wasted if David, Serena or Tiger had been pushed to excel in multiple sports by developing skills in which they showed no promise. The same logic applies to leaders. Focusing on and using your strengths will help you to thrive and excel. This strength-based approach to leadership development recognizes that:

- Leaders have particular strengths which they were either born with or have developed over the years. Such skills come more naturally to them and take less effort to develop.
- They prefer talking about and working on these strengths rather than having to focus on fixing their weaker or non-existent skills.
- It can be demotivating and even stressful for a leader when they're being judged against their weaker areas – like a right-handed person being assessed on their ability to write with their left hand.
- When an organization focuses on helping its leaders develop and use their strengths, the leaders can more easily excel both individually and collectively.

Know your strengths

You probably know where you're talented and strong. If you're unsure, take an online personality assessment which has a strengths-based focus, such as the VIA Character Strengths Assessment or Gallup's StrengthsFinder.

Work with your strengths...

- Always make the time and seek opportunities to deepen and broaden your strengths, ensuring that your skills remain up to date and relevant
- Continually align your career plans so that any leadership job roles you take on are best suited to your skill-set
- This may be a process of trial and error. You may never find a perfect alignment, but avoid job roles in which you can only be successful by excelling in areas in which you're weak and/or have no talent or interest, otherwise you may be setting yourself up for failure.

...and acknowledge your weaker areas

- Decide which weaknesses, if any, are having a material and detrimental impact on your performance as a leader
- Commit to develop these weaker areas or try to change your workload to avoid needing to use those particular skills, for example by delegating certain tasks to other people
- Some leaders choose to change professions or industries to better align their strengths and weaker areas with the requirements of their job role.

Apply the same thinking to your own team

- Help your team grow their own careers by building on and using those skills which are their strengths
- Don't make them feel bad by focusing on their areas of weakness
- Only have them focus on those weaker areas that are essential for their work and career success.

TRUST YOUR INTUITION

'Don't ever ignore your feelings about a situation, decision or person.'

Your gut feelings are a powerful tool to help you successfully lead. Variously referred to as intuition, instinct, vibes, having a feeling or sixth sense, these feelings are your antennae. They give you a sense of what is happening, what the right decision to take is, or what a person is really like. I am sure you must have had many intuitive moments, such as:

- Something does not feel quite right in a business negotiation in spite of everything appearing to be going well
- You're interviewing a candidate with a perfect-looking CV and who answers your questions well, but you have a sense his personality is not ideal for your role
- One of your team members seems very distracted but, when asked, insists everything at work and home is all fine, but you sense otherwise
- You have a feeling that your team members have an issue with each other as they rarely seem to socialize as one team anymore
- Driving to work, you have a flash of inspiration about how to solve a difficult client problem.

Leadership is not easy so, if you have an extra tool to help you, use it. After all, people around you can be hard to read, not always revealing their true intent and feelings, and the business decisions you face are increasingly more complex and challenging. Using your intuition can give you an edge as you try to understand people and make the right decisions.

Listen to your inner voice

The next time you're unsure about something or need to make a choice or decision, give yourself a few seconds to pause and reflect. How do you feel about the person standing in front of you? Does that decision need to be made right now? How does this situation feel in this moment?

Your head is probably guiding you to arrive at an apparently sensible-looking outcome, which might be that the candidate who impressed the most is to be hired, the lowest-cost supplier will be chosen, the most profitable client opportunity will be pursued or the very helpful new colleague is clearly trustworthy. But, before signing off on the decision, ask yourself if your heart agrees with your head and sense how your body feels about the decision. Perhaps you have an uneasy feeling in the pit of your stomach suggesting that something may be amiss, a sense that something is not as it seems. Close your eyes and ask yourself how you really feel, observing what comes to you. It would be okay to decide that you may need more time.

It's easier to sense your inner feelings when you can be free of the noise both around you and inside your head. Try sitting in a quiet place to reflect upon important decisions and to quieten your mind and its hundreds of thoughts and opinions. It may help you to take up meditation and yoga while also spending time in nature, walking in forests or along a beach. Sometimes, it's enough just to sleep on a decision. The morning often brings the answer.

Act upon your gut feelings

Have the courage to follow your intuition even when it might make you stand out and appear odd. Questioning a decision can make you very unpopular. Remember, though, as a leader you're not trying to win a popularity contest – you're always trying to do the right thing even if you're in the minority. Share your feelings and concerns as soon as possible to avoid derailing a decision at the eleventh hour, and also be ready to explain to your colleagues what you're sensing and feeling.

DON'T NEGLECT PRESENTATIONS

'How you present to other people can make or break your business.'

Your leadership happens through communication – spending your time in meetings, writing emails, giving talks, on telephone and video conferences and chatting with people all around you. You'll struggle to perform as a leader if you can't communicate and present well using all of your verbal and non-verbal communication skills.

For most leaders, the hardest type of communication is having to stand up in front of others to make a presentation. I'm sure you've seen people struggling to present in public – choking on their words, sweating and even shaking, never looking at their audience, speaking too softly while trying to get through dozens of boring PowerPoint slides. Many people would love to avoid making presentations, preferring to speak in small groups and communicate over the phone, email or Messenger.

If you want to be a successful leader, however, you can't run away from presenting and must learn to do it well. In a 2016 survey by Prezi and Harris of 2,000 US professionals, almost 70 per cent stated that presentations are critical to their success at work and 75 per cent felt that their presentation skills needed improving.

You might be one of the lucky few who lights up and is a natural when standing on stage facing an audience, and for you making presentations may be straightforward and stress-free. Assuming you're not so fortunate, you need to be ready to hone your skills, build up your confidence and practise. You have no choice if you want to grow as a leader because failing to do so can be detrimental to achieving your goals and to your career – a poor-quality presentation can cause your audience to switch off, lose interest and not buy into your messages. Your reputation in your company might even fall as a result of a poor presentation.

Present like an outstanding speaker

The good news is that presentation skills can be learnt and honed through practice, but it may take time depending upon your current level of confidence and skills. Happily, there are hundreds of talks available online, such as at www.ted.com, so you have easy access to watching and learning from outstanding presenters who have mastered key skills such as the following:

- Controlling body language. It needs to align with the aims of your presentation, and it mustn't act as a distraction. Look around at your audience, make eye contact and smile. Decide whether to sit or stand to present – if the latter, decide whether you will stand still or move around.
- How you look and act when speaking. This sends a message to your audience, so always give time and attention to your choice of clothes, shoes, grooming, make-up and jewellery.
- Showing confidence and demonstrating that you know your subject matter well. You can do this by practising your presentation beforehand so that on the day you're more used to your content and can present more fluently.
- Projecting your voice so that everybody in the audience can hear you. It's always good to speak to the people at the back of the room so that your voice will carry.
- Knowing your audience in terms of their expectations, needs, opinions and likely questions.
- Following the mantra of 'less is more' when deciding the length of your talk, its content, props to be used and the design and number of presentation slides and video clips.
- Giving your talk a clear structure. A good opening, in particular, can capture your audience's interest and so can an impactful closing section.
- Winning over your audience, creating an emotional connection by sharing appropriate personal stories, memories and other personal examples.

OWN UP WHEN YOU'RE WRONG

'Apologising is often viewed as a weakness, when in truth it's a strength.'

I hate to tell you but you can never be a perfect leader. It's impossible to know and understand everything, to always communicate in an ideal way or to make decisions and choices which are always 100 per cent spot on. The best you can do is to continually try to act and say the right things, knowing that sometimes you'll succeed and at other times you'll fall short by making all manner of mistakes. No leader is perfect and there will be many times when you do something wrong:

- You ignore a team member's good suggestions on how to solve a client's problem, only to discover that your own solution made the issue worse
- You promise to revert to your chairperson with an answer to an important question and totally forget to do so
- You insist that your recollection of a meeting's agreed action plan is correct, only to later realize that is isn't
- You insist on choosing who is promoted into a vacant job role but this turns out to be a very poor choice and they have to be fired.

A key measure of your leadership maturity and character is how you respond to your mistakes and setbacks. Too often, leaders will want to hide these mistakes or to blame others, claiming that it's not their fault. A truly successful leader demonstrates courage and humility by being honest and open enough to humbly admit that they were wrong, made a mistake, chose the incorrect direction or used inappropriate words and actions. Be that person.

Step up and be honest

You may be reluctant to admit your mistakes for fear of embarrassment and loss of face, thinking others will view you as being imperfect, weak, poorly prepared or rash. Yes, they might think these things but they will think much worse of you when they discover you were lying about your involvement in an issue. Put aside your ego and discomfort – always come clean.

Never delay acknowledging the obvious

Come clean with both yourself and with those impacted by your mistaken thinking or decision and quickly and methodically plan with colleagues how you'll rectify the issue. You'll gain respect for being open-minded and not allowing your ego and stubbornness to get in the way of saying and doing what's right.

Learn to apologize

Step up and say sorry that you were wrong. Do this in whatever way is most appropriate, which might be by email, during a team meeting or in a larger town hall meeting. In addition to apologising, give due credit and thanks to those who pointed out your mistake.

Openly recognize those colleagues who earlier may have proposed the ideal insights or solutions, which you might have been guilty of overruling or ignoring. Listen to them more next time and pause before shooting them down!

Move on positively

Learn from situations where you were wrong by reviewing your own mindset, assumptions and biases as well as any relevant decision-making, information collation and brainstorming processes to decide what changes you need to make to avoid a repeat.

EMPOWER YOUR TEAM

'When never shown they are trusted and valued, people assume the worst and doubt themselves.'

Most employees want to feel empowered by being supported and encouraged to perform to their highest potential, by being given what they need so that they can achieve their goals without needing constant support, micro-management and hand-holding. Successful leaders know this and always try to empower their teams so that each team member is given:

- The decision-making authority and freedom to complete a project without constantly needing approvals and sign-offs from the boss
- Access to all information needed in order to complete their work without needing to constantly revert for help and advice
- The full authority to hire their own team members and spend money up to agreed limits
- The freedom to solve customer service and client issues without having to seek the boss's approval each time.

The alternative to empowerment is a leader keeping all the control and authority, continually micro-managing the team and making all decisions for them. In such an environment your staff will feel like birds being kept in a cage. Some of your lazier staff may be happy to leave you to make decisions for them, but most people will hate it and many will become demotivated, feel they aren't trusted and that they're prevented from being able to express and be themselves. They will stop trying and going the extra mile by no longer showing any initiative, ownership or creativity. More talented staff will often eventually resign.

Give your team the freedom to act

Consciously step back. Leave your team the space to work independently, take ownership and feel trusted:

- Give your team the necessary written job descriptions, goals and processes which clearly show the degree of freedom and independence they have (e.g. in terms of decision-making and signing authority).
- When possible, delegate to them the full authority to complete their tasks rather than asking them to continually seek your verbal or written approval.
- Adhere to these boundaries – don't be tempted to step in and micro-manage a task you have delegated to them. This can really upset your team.
- Provide all needed resources to enable your team to complete their work independently, with all necessary resources including time, manpower, budgets, tools and equipment and so on.
- Brace yourself for ideas and suggestions coming from your empowered staff. It's inevitable that, when giving people freedom to act, you're also inviting them to share and to speak up. You must positively listen to their ideas and thank them for sharing.
- Although not micro-managing, be ready to step in when asked to provide any guidance, mentoring and feedback to your team members, particularly when they may be doing something for the first time or struggling with challenging parts of their work.
- Openly recognize your team's successes, achievements and results, which they've achieved without your active involvement. Feel proud that you have enabled your team to lead both themselves and their own work.

DON'T NEGLECT THE SMALL TALK

'Leadership is all about successfully interacting with people.'

Your networking and relationship-building skills can make or break your leadership career. This is because your ability to perform as a leader depends on how well you interact with the right people. Maintaining a close connection and relationship with someone can have all kinds of positive consequences:

- Your bank manager might be more open to funding your new business ideas
- A supplier might be more understanding of your temporary cashflow difficulties and let you delay a payment
- Your staff may feel more understood and valued by you and work that little bit more positively
- Shareholders and business partners might be more supportive of your vision and strategy.

Such connections can prove invaluable when you're struggling, perhaps even making serious mistakes or failing to achieve your goals. And colleagues, and other stakeholders with whom you have a strong relationship, might be more open to helping you.

There's no magic number of people that a leader should keep in contact with. The answer depends on your circumstances and on your personality. In any leadership role, there will always be a range of people with whom you should connect in order to achieve all your goals and aims. Some leaders will only need to focus on a small number of relationships, often just their business partner and few key staff.

If you're a quiet, shy introvert, you may be uncomfortable connecting with more people than this. At the other extreme, an outgoing extrovert who loves meeting people might have hundreds of friends and acquaintances. But having a good relationship with someone is not determined by how often you speak together, but instead by factors such as what you have in common, how you're able to help and support each other, and how well you get on. If you worked closely with a colleague in the past, today you might only need to meet or speak with them once a year to maintain the close connection.

Develop your own relationship-building skills

You might be a natural communicator who is happy to walk up to strangers and make small talk. If not, you need to learn how to improve and master whatever skills are necessary to make sure that you build up and maintain important relationships. Perhaps you need to improve in:

- Overcoming your shyness
- Building up your low level of self-confidence
- Being more proactive in trying to connect with new people
- Understanding how to avoid losing touch with people.

Create a stakeholder map

Draw up a list that contains the names of everyone with whom you need to have a working relationship in order to help you succeed as a leader. Known as a stakeholder map, your list will probably be a combination of colleagues, mentors, clients, partners, investors, shareholders, suppliers, key staff, past classmates and other contacts. By each person's name, write a note explaining why you wish to maintain a relationship with them such as: 'because they're senior in my organization' or 'because they're well connected to many of my other stakeholders'. This is a list that you can keep editing and adding to over time.

Decide how to maintain the relationships

For each person, note the possible ways in which it's practical to keep in touch. This might vary from seeing them each day in your office, meeting for a monthly lunch, having a drink on an ad hoc basis, speaking via Whatsapp, meeting when you travel on business, or at an annual alumni event or industry conference. Be systematic in maintaining this to-do list of when and where you'll connect with each person.

DELEGATE WELL

'Only a workaholic superhero is daft enough to do everything themselves.'

Delegation is a really powerful tool to help you succeed in any leadership role. It seems simple to do but is actually extremely difficult to do well. Every day, you have various tasks that need completing. Your challenge is to decide who does what. If you do it yourself, you risk becoming burdened and have no time to perform your other leadership responsibilities. You might be tempted to always delegate tasks to your most able and experienced staff. This might sometimes be best but not always because, as a leader, you need to balance two competing needs:

- To have the work done well through having the most skilled staff completing it in as little time and with as little effort as possible
- To develop and motivate less experienced staff by giving them new tasks to help them master and expand their areas of expertise.

If you only delegate to experienced people, you face two risks:

- Those individuals become overloaded and demotivated, and over time they may even resign
- Your other team members might feel jealous about your perceived favouritism and upset because they never gain the experience and exposure that comes from undertaking those challenging tasks.

Change your delegation patterns

Create an ideal balance between keeping some tasks and delegating others to your experienced and less experienced team members. Why stop there? You may even be able to push some work to other colleagues, perhaps even including your boss!

- Don't delegate tasks to the same few people in your team. Instead, give others the opportunity to learn by taking on this work, recognizing that they may initially struggle. You may need to have a mindset change, away from purely focusing on task completion, and learn to also focus on growing people's capabilities.
- Try rotating who you delegate to by giving different people, each week or month, the opportunity to compete certain tasks, particularly those popular and easier tasks, as well as those that are tedious and boring.
- Stop doing things yourself, because you feel it's quicker and easier. Accept that in the short term it might be more time-consuming to delegate tasks because you need to brief the other person and even help them. But over time, as your team becomes more multi-skilled, you'll be able to pass them work without the need for long explanations or hand-holding.
- Know your team members' strengths, areas of interest, preferences and development needs. With this knowledge, try to make sure that the tasks you delegate to each person are aligned with their wants and needs.
- Beware of always delegating the dirty jobs to your team just because you don't wish to work on these boring, tedious or complicated tasks yourself. This is not a healthy leadership habit and is unlikely to make your team feel good about working under you. Take your share of the drudgery.

INDULGE YOUR CHILD-LIKE CURIOSITY

'Every leader needs to become an open-minded explorer.'

In today's fast changing and increasingly complex world, you can never have all the answers. Fortunately, no one is expecting you to be a leader who knows everything. They are, however, looking to you to lead in finding the most suitable solutions. You're expected to act like a scientist who conducts research and experiments to explore how to improve performance, solve problems or understand why something is happening. A successful leader can appear like a young child who – naturally creative and open-minded – delights in discovering new and previously unknown insights and experiences.

An IBM Global CEO Survey in 2012 collected the views of 1,500 CEOs and found that creativity was the key skill needed to build successful businesses, even more important than qualities such as global thinking and integrity. To foster and enable such creativity takes a combination of you having the right mindset, while creating an environment that enables your colleagues' creativity.

Leaders such as Richard Branson, Jack Ma and Mark Zuckerberg come to mind as well-known examples of such creative leaders who are very open-minded and flexible, and don't stubbornly stick to one idea or direction in the face of better suggestions. They like to try out new ideas, to let their teams run with untried solutions while never viewing any dead ends as wasted effort and a failure, but instead as learning opportunities.

Walk your talk

It's not enough to say that you value and want more creativity and experimentation. The true measure of success comes from whether your staff actually feel they have the space and support to challenge the status quo. Allow your teams to pursue innovative and creative solutions without fearing dire consequences if their efforts fail to yield positive results. You can help create such an environment in a number of ways:

- In team meetings, regularly ask your team if they have alternative solutions and ideas to those on the table. Do this before making any key decisions such as approving a choice of new supplier, a new process, revised organigram or a product solution to meet a client's needs.
- Celebrate as many examples as possible of your employees showing creativity. Do this even when their efforts don't lead to wonderful results that can easily be acted upon.
- Provide the tools and resources your teams need to be creative. This might be as simple as giving them full access to the internet, rather than blocking or filtering apps or web pages for reasons of security or productivity.
- Support the growth of informal sharing networks within your company, which might include colleagues using online platforms in which they share issues and ideas.

Run creativity competitions

Challenge your team or entire organization to suggest ways in which undertaking a particular task or achieving a certain goal can be improved. Invite people to share their ideas no matter how crazy or weird these may appear at first glance. Remember that sometimes a ground-breaking new discovery might have started out as an unusual or unexpected idea. The competition does not need formal prizes although incentives can really motivate people. As a minimum, be ready to publicly acknowledge and thank people for their contributions.

GET YOUR HANDS DIRTY

'There are times when a leader must jump into the muddy trenches to support their team.'

Leadership is never about staying in the same place. It's most definitely not about remaining in your corner office while your team toil away at their workstations. Sometimes you must lead from the front and be with your teams of salespeople, engineers, trainee lawyers, book-keepers, security staff, zero hours contract staff or shop-floor workers. Too many leaders make excuses for not getting involved in this way:

- I don't want to be accused of micro-managing my team
- I delegated all the work to my team, and they are taking full responsibility
- It's not my role to perform their tasks with them
- It's beneath me to get involved in the nitty gritty
- My team don't need me to help them
- I should be focusing my time on higher-level and more strategic tasks.

Spending time with and supporting your team members while they're working is an essential role of any successful leader. The benefits include:

- Understanding first hand the difficulties and challenges facing your team
- Allowing you to better bond and collaborate with your team members
- Helping you see things from your team members' perspectives
- Consciously putting your employees first and showing them respect
- Providing new insights into how efficiency could be improved
- Motivating and engaging your employees, particularly when they see you rolling up your sleeves and helping them with new and challenging tasks.

Rolling up your sleeves also sends a clear message to other leaders with whom you work, encouraging them to learn from and emulate your leadership style. It also serves as a reminder that so much of your organization's success is the result of the commitment and dedication of all your staff, who spend each day facing the customers, manning production lines and doing other essential tasks.

Support, but don't micro-manage

The secret is to spend time with your team, while not becoming a burden through either distracting them from completing their tasks or inappropriately micro-managing them. This is not easy. Simply standing by or sitting with your staff can be off-putting and make them feel that they're being monitored. To minimize this:

- Aim to spend time on the shop floor when you know your team may welcome the extra input. This might be when they're implementing a new process, kicking off a new piece of work or facing a client crisis.
- Plan ahead. Ask your team, in a team meeting, when they might welcome your help.
- If you appear on the shop floor out of the blue, your staff may worry what is wrong, but if you make this a regular habit, they will become more comfortable with your presence.
- Your team may assume that you're offering to help them in order to check and review what they're doing. Be open and honest about your intentions – even if you're not aiming to 'audit' their work, given your wider experience, you may spot mistakes and ways of doing things better. The secret is to not rush to criticize or to make an employee feel inadequate because they missed something that you just spotted.
- Try spending more time with those working a level beneath your direct reports, the level who are sometimes referred to as your N-2s. You could do this through skip-level meetings, where you meet these N-2s without your direct reports being present. The risk is that your direct reports may feel threatened by this. Reassure them that you simply want to better understand their staff, including their work challenges and needs.

DEVELOP YOUR SUCCESSORS

'The true measure of any leader is their gardening skills – how well do they nurture and grow new leaders enabling them to blossom and flourish?'

Creating new leaders should be high up on your to-do list. Just as you were nurtured and prepared for your own leadership opportunities, today's potential leaders now need your care and attention. This is an essential task for any successful leader and was confirmed by the results of the *Global Leadership Forecast 2018* survey by Ernst & Young, DDI and the Conference Board, in which 64 per cent of the surveyed leaders stated that developing their next generation of leaders was one of their top five challenges.

As your business grows in size, it will need more leaders at all levels and you must never assume that this is the sole responsibility of your Human Resources department. It takes a concerted and strategic effort by all leaders to create a large enough pool of leadership talent, and you're best placed to lead in developing new leaders in your own department and job function.

As well as helping your company's future growth, focusing on nurturing and grooming new leaders can have a positive impact on your own career. As an example, you may be missing out on potential job promotions if there are no candidates ready to replace you in your current role. You may also be given lower performance ratings if you're not successfully developing leadership talent within your own team.

Create a leadership pipeline

The key is to have a 'talent pipeline' mentality where you're constantly on the look-out for new and emerging leadership talent and are helping them to grow and rise within your team and organization.

- Invest more of your time and energy in recruiting new staff with potential leadership skills. When interviewing candidates for any positions, look at each person's future potential. Can they grow into any kinds of leadership positions – leading people, projects, businesses or perhaps purely technical leadership?
- Aim to hire only those individuals who will perform their individual and team roles well, while also having the makings of a future leader. Hire and develop people who will be even better than you as a leader – never be threatened by this possibility. Just imagine how amazing your team would perform if it were filled with such talented individuals!
- Understand a team member's leadership potential through observing their personality, attitude and mindset. Look out for generic leadership traits such as initiative, self-responsibility and courage and so on.
- Help your existing team members to develop their own leadership styles and confidence, through mentoring them and allowing them to take on some of your leadership tasks such as chairing certain meetings and leading particular projects. After they have tried their hand at leading these tasks, give them some developmental feedback to help them grow their leadership capabilities.

Not everyone wants to lead

You might want to be a leader, but not everyone does or is suited to managing people, projects or businesses. When creating a leadership development programme and pipeline, be careful not to give the impression to your team that the only measure of success is to be keen and capable of becoming a future leader.

DRIVE FOR RESULTS

'Simply having great ideas and intentions is not enough to ensure success.'

A successful leader knows that their primary role is to achieve some clearly stated goals, no matter the obstacles and hurdles:

- A project manager must complete a project on time, within financial budgets and meeting specific quality targets
- A sales department head must meet sales revenue targets along with goals relating to acquiring new clients, achieving certain profit margins on sales and growing the sales team
- An entrepreneur will have goals such as getting a new product into the market or surviving on available cashflow during an initial start-up phase
- A head of a charity might have fundraising goals as well as targets linked to the charity's aims, such as feeding a certain number of homeless people.

Successful leaders don't just achieve their goals but also aim to exceed expectations by going above and beyond expectations through a combination of determination, having a results-oriented mindset along with the skills to manage necessary tasks, resources, processes and systems. A number of this book's chapters offer you specific advice on doing all of these things well. But there's one skill which comes first and is the most essential – to ensure that the actual goals are created well, that they're both clearly stated and are optimally challenging.

Get buy-in and agreement

No matter whether your goals are referred to as key performance indicators (KPIs), targets or milestones, they need to be clearly stated, understood and agreed upon by everybody who will be involved in achieving them. To achieve this buy-in, you need to be ready to listen, communicate, negotiate and compromise with all relevant parties. This includes with your boss, who might impose some targets on you and your team but which are totally out of reach. You may need to push back and negotiate more acceptable goals and targets.

Cascade goals down to your team

You also need to carefully take any company-wide goals and agree which of these involve you and your team. You need to create and agree any necessary team-wide and individual team member goals which are aligned with the company's.

Set challenging, specific goals

It's a good idea to make the goals for each of your individual team members slightly larger than they need to be, so that the sum of the individual targets exceeds the overall team or department target. Do this so that the chances of you and your team exceeding the overall targets are increased even when some of your team may fall short on their individual targets.

Create and agree SMART goals:

- Specific – specific goals are more easily understood, accepted and achieved.
- Measurable – each goal must be measurable but in terms of how well your team is doing in working towards achieving it.
- Achievable and attainable – the resources including time and people must be made available to enable you and your team to achieve the goal.
- Realistic – a goal should never be impossible to achieve.
- Timely – there must be an understanding and agreement on a goal's time-frame and the deadlines for attaining it.

PUT THE RIGHT PEOPLE IN THE RIGHT ROLES

'Don't force that square shape into a round hole.'

You will rarely have the ideal number of staff each with the perfect mix of soft and hard skills. As a result, you must constantly juggle workloads, priorities and tasks with the available manpower and work with the available talent at your disposal by successfully navigating all kinds of people-related issues:

a. You struggle to fill a key position, perhaps an important technical or specialized sales role, and after a few weeks of interviewing and rejecting unsuitable candidates you're only left with one possible candidate. The problem is that that person only fulfils about 70 per cent of the job's technical requirements.
b. You face a similar issue with your boss, who is urging you to accept a colleague from another department to fill a vacant key role within your team. You know that this individual has a reputation for being very selfish and is a poor team player.
c. Facing a hiring freeze, you can't hire additional staff to work on a new project and your only option is to ask your existing and very busy team members to learn and take on the new project's tasks.
d. Within your team, some people are struggling and seem totally unsuitable for their particular job roles – they may not be very sales, finance or details oriented and so on. You must decide whether to replace them, knowing it will be costly to make them redundant and try to hire replacements.

Successful leaders recognize these dilemmas are not easy to solve. They always try to arrive at ideal outcomes, no matter how difficult or time-consuming it will be. They understand the need for compromises but know that leaving anyone doing work that is not a good fit will always lead to a combination of performance and motivation issues.

Accept compromises with a plan to fill the gaps

Sometimes trying to turn squares into circles will work – one of your team learns to cope with some new and challenging tasks or a weak job candidate you hire works very hard to overcome their weaknesses. But often you'll not be so fortunate and must be creative in how you face each case of not having the right person in the right role. You can only master this over time by facing and learning from many cases.

Let's start by exploring how to deal with the four examples from the previous page:

a. If you do choose to hire the final candidate who only fulfils 70 per cent of the ideal skill-set, plan how to help her plug the 30 per cent gap. This might involve working with your HR colleagues to create a training needs analysis and provide intense technical skills training. In addition, you might spend time mentoring her and asking her colleagues to help her with tasks she is not yet expert in.
b. With the internal candidate who is poor team player, be very careful if you accept him into your team. Be firm in explaining to him your expectations and concerns and then offer to spend time coaching and supporting him to overcome his weak areas in terms of collaborating, sharing and interacting.
c. With the new project example, brainstorm with your team how you can all work smarter to manage the extra workload productively without burning out. Encourage them to write daily to-do lists, spend less time on non-essential tasks and to more proactively support each other.
d. With your poor performers, once you have exhausted all available options to improve their performance, bite the bullet and let them go. Perhaps you could help them transfer internally to take on job roles that are more suited to their skill-sets and preferences. Otherwise, you must be ready to give them notice and fire them.

COACH YOUR TEAM CAREFULLY

'Help your team arrive at their own answers and conclusions.'

Giving your team advice and solutions every time they seek your help can seem like the obvious thing to do. There is, indeed, a time and place for using this very directive leadership style, particularly when:

- Someone new has joined your team and needs lots of guidance
- There's a crisis and your quick decisions and orders are needed to solve an urgent client problem or another emergency situation
- Your team must tackle a new and complicated task or project and only you have the expertise.

However, this must never become your only style when helping your staff solve their problems because when you're giving them answers and being so directive:

- They're not learning to think for themselves and many will feel they're being spoon-fed and become frustrated, while others might enjoy being able to sit back and leave you to do the thinking for them
- You might be giving your team incorrect answers. This may be because you are misunderstanding their problems or issues, and the consequences of your poor advice might have serious consequences.

Successful leaders know when to adopt different styles of conversations and sometimes they adopt a coaching style which involves not providing any answers and solutions, but focuses on asking questions to help colleagues explore and understand their own issues and arrive at their own solutions and answers. You might recall that in chapter 22 you began to learn about coaching.

Have GROW conversations

When your team face challenges and problems, help them to find their own solutions by following a framework known as the GROW model, first created by a coach named John Whitmore:

Goal – start by exploring what the problem, issue, question or challenge is that needs addressing. Ask questions such as:

- What exactly is the issue and why are you trying to focus on it today?
- Why does the issue need solving and what might be a successful resolution?

Reality – help your colleague explore the context, history and background of the issue, through posing questions such as:

- For how long has this been an issue, and who else is aware of it?
- Have you tried resolving it before and what happened?

Options – when you're both clearer on the issue and its context, impact and background, start exploring the options available for solving it by asking:

- If you were alone without my help, what would you do to solve it?
- Do you have a preferred option or many ideas in mind, or are you stuck without a clue of how to move forward?

Way forward – once you have helped your colleague to digest and weigh up any possible options, bring your conversation to a close by asking:

- What will you do now, which option will you proceed with?
- What help or support do you need to implement your chosen way forward?

At the 'options' phase of your GROW conversation, and only after the other party has shared their own options, do offer to share any additional ideas based on your insights and experience. Share them but don't tell the person which option is best and instead help them to reach their own conclusions.

PERSIST WHEN OTHERS GIVE UP

'How tragic to turn back and, through clearing skies, you realize that you had been so close to the mountain's summit after all.'

Too many leaders give up just short of achieving their plans, goals or dreams, thinking that they have exhausted all avenues, hit dead ends and used up all of their ideas, energy and resources. Successful leaders never throw in the towel so quickly. Instead, they persist knowing that any goal worth achieving is not going to be easy.

In today's fast changing and disruptive VUCA business environment, where businesses are struggling to adapt and even survive, we should not be surprised if our goals and targets can seem more challenging than in the past and may even seem impossible to achieve. As a result, the tendency to want to give up will be high and even successful leaders might struggle to remain persistent and keep going.

In addition to helping achieve business goals, not giving up too easily can also benefit your career. According to a 1985 research paper, more persistent leaders tend to be viewed more favourably. The author of the paper, US academic professor Laura M. Graves, found that leaders who exhibited persistence were evaluated and rated more highly than non-persistent leaders. This makes sense and I am sure that you too have more admiration and respect for colleagues who show more willingness to persist and never give up, compared to those who more easily quit.

Develop your determination muscles

Build up your persistence by developing your willpower and determination:

- Constantly remind yourself and your team why a goal is important for you and your organization. Try discussing and visualizing the positive impacts and benefits of achieving that particular goal.
- Avoid being distracted by things you can't control. Instead, focus your energy on those tasks that you and your team can influence and change.
- Don't allow negative or demotivated people to affect you.
- A large goal can easily seem too daunting and difficult to achieve compared to smaller ones. Break down any longer-term and larger goals into a series of smaller ones.
- Celebrate achieving each of these smaller goals to help motivate you and your team as you work towards the larger goal or target.
- Ask a trusted colleague to hold you accountable and encourage you to stay the course, speaking with them when you're doubting yourself and feeling tempted to give up with a piece of work. You, in turn, can provide the same support to your own team members.

...and recognize when you SHOULD give up

Your new found willpower and persistence should only be used when needed and not all the time. Sometimes you really do need to give up and stop chasing a goal when it's clearly no longer achievable or your priorities have changed and that goal is no longer relevant.

CONTROL YOURSELF

'If you want to quickly fail as leader, simply start losing your cool.'

You would become very irritated if your oven had no temperature control and would randomly leave your food under- or over-cooked, just as you would be frustrated if your fridge had a broken thermostat leaving you with rotten food one day and solid and frozen milk the next. We feel the same when a colleague has no self-control, and it's even worse when it's the leader because anything they say or do can have a large impact on so many people.

At the start of this book, I spoke about the importance of self-leadership and a key aspect of this is how well you control yourself. This is sometimes referred to as self-management, which forms part of your emotional intelligence (EQ), a concept I explained in chapter 33. Successful leaders know that excellent self-management is essential. Without it, you risk making all kinds of horrible and sometimes repetitive mistakes that can have all kinds of consequences:

- You repeatedly lose your temper about trivial and small mistakes made by your team, and some of your team members may become so upset by your reaction that they resign.
- You have a couple of drinks and make inappropriate comments about a work colleague, and as a result you're investigated by your HR department and risk losing your job.
- You become upset by an email from a client who is blaming your team for poor performance and you reply with a strong and very emotional email.
- During a management meeting, in response to someone challenging you, you become angry and start a heated argument, causing one colleague to say they're tired of having to work with you.

Follow a simple process of self-control

- Observe yourself more closely and learn when you're becoming emotional and liable to act without thinking.
- Ask trusted colleagues you're working with to warn you when they sense you might be losing your cool.
- When you're on the verge of saying the wrong thing, pause and excuse yourself from a meeting, or silently count to ten to calm yourself.
- When you realize too late and you have already said or done something inappropriate, immediately apologize to those impacted by your words or actions.

Take care with your emails and phone calls

If you know you're upset while writing an email, don't immediately send it. Save it as a draft and come back to it later and decide whether it's okay to send. Similarly, when on the phone or in a video conference, when becoming riled up and upset, find an excuse to pause the conversation, maybe asking for a toilet or coffee break – this will give you time out to calm down.

Seek anger management counselling

Sometimes the only way of bringing your emotions under control is to seek counselling from a trained therapist with whom you can explore what is triggering your reactions. They can help you overcome any underlying insecurities, past events and traumas that are fuelling your behaviours.

Avoid being tired, stressed or hungry

You'll find self-control easier on a full stomach, after a good night's sleep and when you've exercised and are free of stress. Without enough sleep and healthy eating, your brain will become less sharp and clear and you risk becoming easily irritated, tired and short-tempered, which increases the probability of you losing your control with other people.

KEEP YOUR VALUES CENTRE STAGE

'What you value in life dictates what kind of leader you become.'

A successful leader is continually striving to live and lead with some carefully chosen values. Also known as principles or standards, your values underpin how you think, make decisions, act and behave as a leader. They are what drive you and what you seek when leading both yourself and other people. Some people have no idea what their values are but successful leaders always know what is driving them. Their values might include:

Appreciation	Fairness	Learning
Authenticity	Focus	Making a difference
Autonomy	Freedom to act	Optimism
Belief	Gratefulness	Passion to win
Caring	Helping	Purpose
Commitment	Humility	Respect
Compassion	Inspiring	Transparency
Courage	Integrity	Truth
Empathy	Loyalty	Trust
Excellence	Lead by example	Wisdom

A leader's values help them know what kinds of behaviours are and are not acceptable to them:

- When a leader values integrity, they will react strongly when a colleague lies or cheats.
- A leader who values being caring and empathic will often be the first to console and support a team member who is very upset.
- The leader for whom persistence is an important value will rarely give up with challenging tasks even when everybody else has done so.

Discover your values

The easiest way to know what your values are is to list the actions and behaviours of other people that make you angry or upset:

- When a colleague upsets you by never preparing for meetings or can never find important paperwork, you probably value work qualities such as being prepared and being organized.
- When a team member annoys you by always rushing to speak and to dominate discussions, it might be a sign that you value calm reflection and allowing others to be heard.

To also help you discover what is important to you, ask close colleagues to describe your working style, attitudes and behaviours, and what they have observed as being very important to you.

Focus on only the values that serve you

Once you know your values, reflect upon which ones are helpful to you as a leader. These are the ones you should focus on and might include positive qualities such as being unselfish, empathic, bigger-picture focused and inspirational. Encourage your team to practise these same values – if they do, they will eventually become the team's daily habits and working culture.

...and stop focusing on those that are out of date

Some of your values might be hindering you today as a leader. They might have helped you in the past when you were an individual contributor or were in a different work environment. But now you realize they're no longer helpful, stop treating them as something you value and do. Such 'out of date' values might include qualities such as independence and working alone, being a perfectionist or being very expressive and emotional.

OPTIMISE EVERYTHING

'There's always room for improvement with every single thing you touch.'

Sometimes you must act like a management consultant by working with your colleagues to help discover more optimal ways of doing things and lead the implementation of any agreed changes or upgrades to systems, processes or procedures. The resulting discoveries might generate huge benefits in terms of productivity gains, cost reductions and shorter timeframes.

As a leader, you have a good overview of what your different team members and colleagues need to do and achieve, as well as what the systems, workflow and processes are that they must follow. As a result, you're well placed to observe and understand when:

- Work flows may seem over-complicated and inefficient
- Processes seem to bring little or no value or are being replicated
- Systems and procedures cause unnecessary bottlenecks and delays
- Some excellent work flows and systems could be replicated in other areas of the business
- There are gaps and things missing, being ignored or not being done well.

Successful leaders are used to spotting and discussing such areas for improvement, evaluating how solutions might be implemented. Over time, they're able to develop a systematic and process-driven frame of mind while also maintaining a bigger-picture view and a details-oriented focus. They understand it's a team effort and that so much more can be discovered when working together, even involving newer hires, who may bring a fresh perspective and child-like curiosity to your team.

Understand best-practice ideas and tools

Take an interest in research and articles written by well-known global management consultancies such as Mckinsey, Bain, Stategy+ and PwC, which offer insights into how leaders are changing and optimizing different aspects of their organizations.

Invest time in becoming familiar with the range of tools, methodologies and frameworks used by leaders and their teams, which can be used to discover, plan and implement optimal organizational changes and improvements. The more popular tools today include:

- Agile – this is a process for making improvements where small cross-functional teams take full accountability for issues they're asked to tackle.
- Scrum – this is related to Agile and involves work being undertaken by small teams who divide the tasks into work that can be completed in short and defined time periods.
- Kanban – a process of visualizing processes and workflow to identify potential bottlenecks and solutions to fix them.
- 6 Sigma – a range of processes used to identify and eliminate the causes of errors or defects and to reduce variability in the quality of any kind of business process.
- Waterfall – this refers to work being broken down into tasks, with each task depending on a previous one being completed.
- Kaizen – this refers to a process of continuously seeking to make lean improvements in any part of an organization.

Be okay with any disruption

No matter how disruptive and painful a new and needed process might be to implement and work with, always keep in mind and remind your staff of the benefits that may be created and implemented as a result. Think of any disruption like a major road works – irritating in the short term in return for faster and easier traffic flows in the future.

SENSE-CHECK BEFORE YOU ACT

'Better to ask a silly question today than to make a stupid mistake tomorrow.'

When is the last time that you totally misunderstood something, failing to make sense of what you observed, understood or were told?

There's nothing worse than finishing an important task feeling that you've done a great job only to discover that you'd misunderstood what you needed to do, and that your time and effort were wasted. This can be both embarrassing and costly, as you may need to start the task all over again or may have missed an opportunity or key deadline and it's too late to redo the work. This can really annoy and demotivate your team if they must help you rework things. In extreme cases, your misunderstanding might cost you your reputation or even career.

Junior employees might be forgiven for making such mistakes and the cost of them doing the wrong thing is hopefully small. As a leader, you're being paid to get things right and not to create more problems by not understanding properly what needs to be done. Successful leaders totally understand this and, to ensure they're never guilty of the same mistake, they:

- Spend time making sense of what they're being asked to do, the questions they need to answer or problems they may need to solve.
- Do the same with their teams and colleagues, encouraging them to explore what they're hearing and understanding while also questioning their own assumptions and perceptions.

Put it into action

52

Slow down to make sense of things

Before rushing to answer and solve issues and problems, always spend time alone or with colleagues to make sure that you fully understand what is happening and what is being asked or expected of you and your team. I call it slowing down to speed up. Those extra few minutes or days of delay before starting a task can make all the difference. It's comparable to reading instructions before perfectly assembling one of those DIY pieces of furniture. We all know what happens if you rush to assemble without referring to the instructions at all and getting bits of wood back to front!

Take care when a colleague quickly responds in a meeting saying, 'Yes, I understand and it's no problem, I will get started right away.' Sometimes that might be right response but so often it won't be the case. Start being a leader who is always helping others to make sense of things by asking questions such as:

- It might be a silly question but are we sure about our assumptions or about what the client is really asking us to do?
- At the risk of sounding stupid, is it really as simple as we are making the problem sound?
- Do we need to double check what the other department is expecting?

WALK TALL

'You can't successfully lead when you're cowering in the corner of the room.'

When you meet new people, do they sense and acknowledge you're a leader, doing so before you introduce yourself and exchange name cards? So many leaders lack presence, gravitas and stature. When they walk into a meeting with some of their team, other people never guess they're the boss, perhaps mistaking a more confident and extrovert colleague of theirs for that role.

You may feel comfortable not standing out as a leader and be very happy to have your colleagues seen as more senior than you. In fact, sometimes this can be a good thing, for example during a key negotiation when you want to quietly observe the other party without them knowing who you are.

However, most of the time, you can't hide away in this manner because to successfully perform in your role you need appear as and act like a leader. You need to do so in order to stand up for your team and company and represent both in all kinds of meetings, negotiations, venues and events. To do this well, you need executive presence, also referred to as gravitas, stature or walking tall. It's not easy to master but successful leaders always work to acquire such gravitas. Some are luckier than others and, by virtue of their personality, physical appearance, language skills or upbringing, they may have a natural executive presence. If you're not so fortunate, you must learn and practise a few tips.

Own the role you're in

Perhaps you shy away and lack the confidence to act like a leader because you feel you don't deserve to be in the leadership position in the first place. Known as imposter syndrome, this tendency to feel you're not ready for or worthy of your current job role is quite a common anxiety. On average, I sense it affects women more than men. Talk about your issue with close colleagues, asking them to encourage and mentor you to become comfortable in your role.

...then build up your extrovert confidence

If not already an outgoing and communicative extrovert, learn how to be one. Start by building up the confidence to say hello to new people, make small talk and give presentations as well as an experienced presenter. You might initially feel reluctant, particularly if you're a shy introvert, but all you can do is practise each day so that, little by little, you become more comfortable being outgoing and more confident in presenting yourself to other people.

...and literally stand tall and dress the part

Body language and posture sends a very strong message and by simply standing upright in a calm way, you project more gravitas and stature. Similarly, what you wear has an impact on how you appear. It's worth the effort to find out what clothes, accessories and hairstyles work best for you in your particular work environment.

GIVE OTHERS THE SPOTLIGHT

'Never hog the limelight.'

One of your main roles as a leader is to motivate people, including by making sure that they're acknowledged, thanked and recognized. This can bring so many benefits to you and them:

- People are happier, more satisfied and productive when their boss and colleagues are talking about and acknowledging their successes.
- As their boss, you should also feel energized because your team will admire and respect you more because of how you value and recognize them.
- It's easier to give someone critical feedback or ask them to take on difficult tasks when you have already created a strong relationship, based on you regularly recognizing their positive qualities and good work.

Recognition can take many forms from a simple 'thank you' in a meeting, through having them share at your annual company conference about a project they have successfully worked on, awarding them the employee of the month, all the way to offering them a job promotion.

When recognition is lacking, people can get very upset. Perhaps you have experienced how this feels when you have been similarly ignored – you probably started to become demotivated, disengaged, even depressed and feeling worthless. People can feel especially upset when they see others getting the recognition for work that they themselves were wholly or partly responsible for. This can lead to anger, envy, jealousy and even complaints that their boss is showing favouritism or being mean in denying them any recognition.

Vary how you recognize people

Giving recognition is not as simple as doing one thing all the time. Too much of the same thing loses its impact and there's a limit to how many times a person can be given the same employee of the month award before it begins to feel awkward and embarrassing.

Similarly, you can't hope to recognize different people in the same way. One person might really appreciate a 'thank you' email written about them and sent to a wider team, while for another this might mean very little and they may be seeking recognition in terms of more job responsibilities.

Take time in your working week to reflect about who needs recognition and the forms it might take. Be generous and fair and avoid accusations of always recognizing the same few people in your team. Try asking your team members if they feel that you're recognizing them enough and for the right reasons, and involve them in suggesting who may be worthy of some special recognition.

Create opportunities for recognition

Always give people the opportunity to shine and to stand in the limelight and, when possible, sacrifice your own opportunity or need to be recognized:

- When senior bosses are visiting your department or location, allow your team to meet and present to them without you doing all the talking.
- When you're asked to represent your team at a global annual event, don't always attend yourself but ask one of your team to stand in for you. Consciously rotate who you ask each time such an opportunity arises to be able to give the limelight to more people.

WISELY STEP IN TO MICRO-MANAGE

'Breathing down their necks is unlikely to endear you to your team, but sometimes you just have to.'

One of the worst types of leader is the one who never leaves their team members alone. In chapter 43, you learnt that being a boss who is guilty of peering over your team's shoulders can be very demotivating and suffocating, and is often a key reason why someone resigns from their job.

Although micro-managing must never be your default leadership style, sometimes you have to micro-manage when you know there are very good reasons to become very closely involved in a team member's work. These might include when:

- A new team member has joined the team who is not familiar with various aspects of their duties and responsibilities.
- An existing and experienced team member has taken on a new and challenging task that may be very high profile or very costly if not done well.
- You have a poor-performing team member who you need to work closely with in an attempt to encourage and challenge them to improve.
- There's an emergency or very urgent deadline and you know you can't risk leaving your staff alone to deal with the relevant tasks. Such periods of firefighting are hopefully rare and not a daily occurrence.

Choose carefully when you micro-manage

The secret is to never allow any form of micro-managing to become your default habit and automatic style but instead to have it as one of the possible tools that you only use in very specific situations where you feel it's the most appropriate leadership style.

Be an encouraging and inspiring micro-manager

The difficult thing about micro-managing is doing so without demotivating and upsetting staff. Successful leaders manage this by following these rules:

- Explain your reasons and need to work closely with them and ask for your team member's understanding.
- Ask them how they would like to be micro-managed rather than simply imposing your style on them. They may prefer to come to your office rather than having you peering into their work area.
- Remain calm and avoid showing unnecessary anxiety, stress and worry (about the person's performance) as this will make the other person more anxious and they may start to view your attempts to help them in a negative light.
- Show that you value and trust the person you're micro-managing. This is not easy as being micro-managed leaves most people with a sense of not being trusted. Try to overcome this by openly talking with your team members about how much you trust and value them, explaining the reasons why you need to micro-manage them at this point.

SPREAD OPTIMISM

'Be careful what you start – both optimism and pessimism are highly contagious.'

Have you ever worked for a very pessimistic boss? There can be nothing worse than working for someone who is always grumpy, negative and depressed. You'll feel demotivated and unhappy while your boss will probably underperform in their leadership role. Common sense suggests such a correlation between a leader's optimism and their performance, and a 2017 research paper in the *International Journal of Management* that reviewed studies on this topic confirmed this, finding that optimism strongly impacts leadership effectiveness in four ways:

- Optimism creates trust between people
- It helps a leader remain positive and resilient in troubled times
- It creates a more cooperative and sharing environment
- It raises a person's self-efficacy or belief in their ability to achieve goals.

But optimism does more than even this. It can also help you achieve a healthier and longer life! A 2002 Yale University study concluded that more positive people live an average of 7.6 years longer than other people do. So it's worth working on...

Successful leaders understand all of these benefits and will always try to project optimism, knowing that being pessimistic and down will only serve to demoralize your employees, turn away clients and even make investors cautious.

There are moments though when an experienced leader might need to tone down appearing so optimistic, for example when apologizing for a mistake their company has made, announcing poor financial results or acknowledging the death of a colleague. But these are exceptions that prove the rule, most of the time a successful leader will consistently project optimism in all their words and actions.

Develop an optimistic outlook

Train your mind to be optimistic, whether you're a naturally positive person or are someone who tends to view the glass as being half empty.

- Have an honest look at your patterns and ask other people to give you their opinions on how often and in what ways you exhibit a positive and optimistic outlook.
- Understand when you may have a tendency to act the opposite, for example when things are not going your way or someone is disagreeing with you. Ask close colleagues to tell you when they observe you starting to act in a negative way. Tell yourself in that moment to let go and move on, by smiling, laughing, taking a walk or closing your eyes and calmly observing yourself breathe. If necessary, be an actor and fake a smile.
- Approach events and situations through a positive lens by asking yourself and your colleagues questions such as, 'In spite of this delay, what are the positives we can build on?', 'Although we are facing these roadblocks, what is going well?' or 'The project may have failed to meet the client's expectations but what are the positive lessons learnt for next time?'
- Stay away from negative people and avoid hiring such people into your teams and organization. Their lack of positive mindset can be toxic and will sap your energy as you try to manage and ring-fence their negativity.
- Always inform your team members and colleagues when you're not feeling positive and may come across as negative or depressed. When feeling this way, try to stay away from people by working from home, cancelling meetings and avoid making important decisions. When feeling down, it's better to be alone rather than allow other people to catch a dose of your pessimism!

PICK PEOPLE UP WHEN THEY FALL

'Everybody faces struggles. Leadership is about encouraging people to keep on trying.'

It's very easy for a leader to acknowledge and celebrate their team's successes, particularly when they can share in the glory. The team's good work reflects well on you as their boss and you'll be easily motivated to share, build on, sustain and replicate these successes.

Your challenge arises when the opposite happens and one of your team struggles to achieve their goals and might even completely fail. In today's increasingly volatile and complex business environment, struggling and failing are becoming more common. How will you respond when it happens?

How you react to your team members when they fail at something is an important measure of your leadership maturity. It can be very easy to simply become angry, upset and critical and to leave your team member in no doubt as to what they have done wrong. A wise leader might also be upset but would quickly switch to a broader strategy of helping the individual to learn, grow and move forward through:

- Challenging them to accept, learn and grow from their experiences and mistakes
- Supporting them to positively move forward and to keep on trying.

Systematically challenge and support

Whenever one of your team struggles to complete their work and achieve their goals, use this five-part process to help them learn and grow:

1. Allow the individual to talk about and share their feelings, disappointments and concerns (e.g. over how people, including you, reacted).
2. Support them to explore, understand and learn from what happened, who was at fault and how to avoid repeating the same mistakes.
3. Provide necessary training, coaching, mentoring or other forms of support to help them succeed next time.
4. Spend time with them encouraging, inspiring, uplifting and motivating them to confidently and positively move on.
5. Give them the backing, trust and reassurances to encourage them to undertake the same activity or task again.

Never gloat

Never be a leader who revels in other people's struggles and failures, even if they're your competitors. Stay silent and neutral if you must, but never put someone else down when they're already feeling bad and struggling. Apart from being the right thing to do, you never know when you may need their help, encouragement and support in the future...

When mistakes are repeated, respond with wisdom, not emotion

If somebody repeats the same mistake, you may feel upset and angry with them. Depending on the circumstances, you may wonder if you should retain this person in your team. Before blaming them, explore whether their struggles might in fact be your fault and that you:

- Did not do all you could to help them learn from their first mistake
- Did not optimally equip and support them to try again another time.

NO BULLSHIT ALLOWED

'Want to be a great leader? Start by cutting out the lies.'

Leaders are continually being shown to have lied. Too often, it's shrugged off and accepted with all kinds of justifications such as:

- 'It was a small twisting of the truth.'
- 'Other people make the same false claim.'
- 'It was a one-off and I never normally deceive people.'
- 'The truth is too painful and complicated.'
- 'Everyone else is saying the same thing.'
- 'The truth is so unclear anyway.'
- 'Nobody wants to hear the truth.'

You might feel that telling the occasional lie is acceptable and insist that you're honest the rest of the time. However, a 2016 study in the *Nature Neuroscience* journal in which a team of psychologists, including Dan Ariely, showed that as we lie more, our brains produce fewer feelings of guilt, fear and anxiety. In other words, as we act more dishonest and deceptive, we become less likely to stop ourselves doing it again.

Trying to be honest may not be easy but the benefits should be incentive enough to compel you to try to always act with 100 per cent integrity:

- You'll be trusted and respected as someone who speaks the truth and gives honest feedback and assessments. There may be moments when you're not very popular for speaking the truth but others will hopefully respect you for being a person of character.
- Honesty is so easy while lying takes energy because you have to expend energy not being found out. This involves having to remember what you said in case you ever need to repeat the same lie.
- People will be more comfortable in opening up and sharing with you when they know you can be trusted to keep your word.
- Being honest is contagious and will encourage those you work with to also be more open and truthful.

Think long-term reputation over short-term gains

The next time you're tempted to tell even a small white lie, ask yourself 'Is the cost of being found out really worth it?' Even if your conscience is fine with you twisting the truth, is your reputation and name going to withstand the discovery that you were dishonest?

You need to be especially strong when coming under pressure from colleagues to cover something up and to lie – such as pretending a task was completed on time when it was not. Be strong and understand that protecting your reputation must always outweigh the upset and pressure that you cause by refusing to play along.

If it becomes too stressful to remain honest, be willing to move on. Choosing to resign is never a failure in such cases and is simply you choosing to protect yourself from potential bullying, peer pressure and being ostracized by your colleagues. If you're a senior leader and feel strong enough, you may choose to stay in order to try to proactively change the working culture.

Push others to come clean

Even if you work in a really healthy environment where integrity is highly valued, you may still have colleagues who make up stories and play with the truth from time to time. As a leader, it's your duty to stop them in their tracks. You may try to do this diplomatically, in private, in a friendly unofficial manner or in a more formal way where you officially report what they have done.

DON'T FORGET YOUR HEALTH

'It's not easy to lead other people when lying in a hospital bed or in a coffin!'

Nobody would destroy their health in pursuit of leadership and career success, would they? Sadly, far too many leaders do exactly this. They work their way up the leadership ladder while simultaneously burning out from stress, becoming physically sick, mentally ill and emotionally drained. I have coached dozens of such leaders and am astonished how unhealthy they had allowed themselves to become while chasing year-end bonuses and promotions.

Successful leadership requires skills such as details orientation, concentration, emotional balance, focus, calmness and persistence, all of which require you to be at your best. When you're stressed, overloaded and worn out, you can't perform these things well and as a result you risk:

- Making poor decisions and other mistakes because you're tired and unable to concentrate
- Lacking positive inspiration due to feeling stressed and depressed
- Not being calm and happy because of the pain and irritation from tense muscles, a stiff neck or headaches
- Having no desire to look forward, to set a vision and direction because you're so drained. As a result, you may start losing interest in your work and career.

Look after all parts of your health

You must do whatever it takes to maintain your overall well-being and health:

- Physical health – have an exercise regime made up of physical activities that interest you such as walking, running, sports or visits to the gym.
- Mental health – keep your mind calm and rested by seeking moments of silence, stepping away from the noise of your everyday tasks, perhaps taking up meditation and taking walks in nature.
- Emotional health – step away from tense and angry situations and pause before reacting when a person or situation is making you boil inside.
- Spiritual health – we all seek meaning in our work and balance in our lives. When your leadership role no longer gives you either, make changes. This might include moving on from your current job and/or organization.

Always put your health ahead of your leadership career

When the stresses of being a leader gets the better of you, be willing to step back, slow down or even resign to protect your health. This is what successful leaders do and you should never feel you have failed by putting your health ahead of your career. Take a leaf out of the book of Lloyds Bank's CEO, Antonio Horta-Osorio, who temporarily stepped down from his role in 2011 to recover from exhaustion. After a couple of months of leave, he returned to his leadership role with the bank, which he still holds.

Keep an eye on your team's health

Help your team to focus on their own health by talking about health-related topics and issues such as stress, working hours, conflicts and tensions, physical working environments, healthy eating and exercise. Always be supportive of your employees' ideas and suggestions relating to ways in which you can collectively make all of your work and lives healthier.

BE BOLD AND DARING

'Stop playing it safe. Take your team where you have never been before.'

Your leadership skills will be tested when you're taking your team, organization or business in new and uncharted directions in pursuit of some large and audacious goals. Too many leaders are too cautious and conservative to do this and will find every imaginable reason to explain why such goals are impossible to achieve.

Successful leaders are quite different and never suppress their boldness, passion, audacity and daring. They use these things to excite, energize and motivate people (including themselves) to tackle even the most impossible looking goals. You can always spot such leaders as the ones who:

- Are willing to create and focus on extraordinary goals that might seem like pipe dreams to others
- Turn ordinary teams into extraordinary team players who are happy to commit to challenges that would overwhelm most people.

Elon Musk is an example of a leader who consistently acts in this bold and daring way. You can see this in all of his projects and businesses including in his plans to colonize Mars, to create re-usable vertical landing rockets and to build the world's largest lithium-ion storage system in South Australia in a self-imposed short time-frame. Not every leader has the personality, ambition or inclination to become an Elon Musk, but all successful leaders do develop and practise, in their own way, the skills of thinking big and encouraging others to follow suit.

What is stopping you from thinking big?

Observe your reactions and feelings when presented by your colleagues or senior bosses with a very ambitious goal or dream. If you're reluctant to explore and embrace their ideas, understand why and be willing to work out why you're reluctant:

- It's okay to feel overwhelmed and worry about the challenges involved in working on such goals. But this is an issue to deal with later, not a reason to shoot down the ambitious goal or plan today.
- It's understandable to think a large goal may be impossible to achieve and, as a result, to not want to invest any time or energy in discussing it.
- But suspend such scepticism and disbelief, saying to yourself 'maybe it's possible' and start allowing yourself to actively listen to those who are selling the idea.

Take the risk to chase enormous goals

Be willing to pursue your own bold goals. Just as you might have been sceptical of other people's ambitious and crazy ideas, be ready to develop a thick skin to repel other people's doubts and scepticism. Become so passionate about your own ideas that you can more easily find the courage and sense of conviction to push ahead, even when your colleagues may think you're crazy.

Seek buy-in from your team

- Practise being more extrovert and expressive in your communications. This will help give uplifting, inspiring and motivational talks to your team to seek their support for your goals.
- Use positive and inspiring words such as calling your plans exciting, ground-breaking and first of a kind to help enthuse your colleagues and help them buy into your ideas.
- You could also create stories to share with your team that help express the vision of where you wish to take them, and make it easier for them to understand your bold goals.

LOOK WAY BEYOND THE BOTTOM LINE

'Every leader has a deep purpose and responsibility to the earth and all humanity.'

It's no longer enough to meet your sales, profits and growth targets. To call yourself a successful leader today, you also need to ensure that everything you create is sustainable and helping make the world a healthier and better place in which to live. To do this, you need to recognize and deal with all kinds of questionable leadership practices with which you might be connected, such as:

- Building up a highly profitable mineral water business which is removing all of the water from the local aquifers and reducing the water table
- Expanding your purchasing of clothing products from suppliers in low labour-cost countries and turning a blind eye to claims that your clothes are produced with child and forced labour and produce dye waste that pollutes rivers by the factories
- Happily distributing single-use coffee pods and other plastic-based products without having any plans to move to biodegradable products or having product recycling initiatives with your customers
- Outsourcing your warehousing and supply chain to a firm whose staff are on zero hours contracts and who must stand continuously for 12-hour shifts with only very short monitored breaks
- Having a high carbon footprint through allowing your staff to always fly to conduct business rather than working through video conferences with overseas colleagues and stakeholders
- Running a furniture manufacturing firm which sources wood from logging companies who are felling trees without any regard for the environmental impact.

You can no longer lead a business in isolation and ignore its impact on the environment, communities and society at large. So no matter whether you lead a small local or large global organization, become a leader who wants to leave a positive impact on the world around you for the future of your children and their children.

Review where your business is today

Carry out an audit of your entire business practices, processes and leadership decisions using external consultants or drawing upon a cross-section of staff and leaders to conduct the review. Have them draw up a list of any questionable activities and organize brainstorming and feedback sessions to collectively decide ways in which your business can be more ethical, fair and environmentally friendly.

Try the 'what would your 16-year-old think?' test

To give you a wider perspective, share the results of your audit and of the brainstorming and feedback sessions with a group of young people. Ask them what they think you should do. It's highly likely that they will answer you from a very clear ethical, sustainable and fair standpoint and that their conclusions may help steer your own decision-making.

Have regular CSR discussions

Get into the habit of having corporate and social responsibility (CSR) reviews and conversations involving a wide cross-section of your company's staff and key stakeholders. Create a budget for spending on various CSR-related initiatives such as giving back to the local community, organizing beach clean-ups and creating recycling systems.

Have the courage to sacrifice the bottom line

Never delay rectifying unacceptable practices. It's better to face the cost and pain by choice, rather than waiting for a scandal to force the company to change. Become a leader for whom profits are important but not everything. Make it clear that you would never hesitate to do what is right and incur the extra cost. An example might be to stop buying raw materials from low-cost factories that treat their staff badly, and switch to more expensive suppliers who are being openly monitored and provide fairer working conditions to their staff.

BE AN EXCELLENT MENTOR

'To help other people grow, share your words of wisdom.'

All leaders share their expertise, knowledge and experiences and by doing so are being mentors to their colleagues (who, in mentoring jargon, are mentees). Unfortunately, most leaders do this very badly because they have never been taught how to professionally mentor other people. Their most common mistakes include:

- Sharing favourite stories and anecdotes from their careers that may have no relevance to what a mentee's challenges are and what they're seeking help with
- Lecturing a mentee without asking any questions to better understand the mentee's actual needs or to clarify if the mentee is understanding what is being said
- Not listening to the mentee and treating the mentoring as a one-way communication process and an opportunity to show off and impress
- Learning nothing from the mentee's own experiences.

Poor mentoring is counter-productive and can leave a mentee struggling to find value in and apply the advice the leader has given them. The resulting confusion and sense of being stupid can be very demotivating and disengaging. This is comparable to a leader always being directive through telling, lecturing and teaching and their staff just have to listen.

Best practice mentoring is not simply about giving other people your advice, experience and opinions, it's a journey of discovery involving:

- A two-way sharing and learning process, in which the mentor helps the mentee reflect upon their own experiences, build up their own wisdom, become mature and improve the depth and breadth of their thinking.
- The mentor asking insight-provoking questions rather than simply giving advice. At appropriate moments, they may draw upon their own experiences and share helpful insights and suggestions aligned with the mentee's own needs, situation and context.

Become a best-practice mentor

Adopt the following framework for responding to requests for help:

- When asked to help someone, first decide whether they need an immediate answer from you or whether there's time to mentor.
- Start any mentoring as a coaching conversation by exploring what the mentee's issues are and what options they already have in mind to solve their own problems. To help guide the conversation, follow the GROW model which you learnt in chapter 47.
- During the conversation, switch from coaching to mentoring by saying something like: 'Having helped you explore and understand your issue and available options, let me share some helpful ideas and suggestions...'
- Align your advice with your colleague's own situation and needs. Ask the mentee whether they found your idea or story helpful and relevant, and how might they apply it to their own setting.
- If both of you find the initial mentoring conversation of value, you could continue the relationship over many months, having further conversations where the mentee can bring up any topic for discussion.

Create an in-house mentoring programme

Work with your HR colleagues to set-up (or offer to support any existing) in-house mentoring programmes where newer and/or less experienced staff and leaders can be paired with a mentor such as yourself. Ideally a person's mentor should never be their own line manager (in order to give the mentee someone other than their boss to open up to).

Be open to learning from your mentees

Younger team members might bring you all kinds of new insights, including in the areas of technology, and trends among their generation that might help you learn how to motivate and engage with them. This process of a mentor learning from a mentee is known as reverse mentoring.

BREAK RULES

'Show bravery by ignoring silly rules and norms.'

Successful leaders sometimes don't allow rules, policies and norms to stand in their way of taking the right actions, choices and decisions.

The larger and more established the organization you work within, the more likely that rules might have to be bent or ignored in order to get things done. This might involve breaking accepted norms, unwritten rules, agreed policies or written guidelines such as:

- Your predecessor always attended particular weekly internal meetings but you realize that there's no point in you continuing this practice and you stop attending. When challenged on why you're breaking this accepted practice, you may have to explain your reasoning.
- HR policies state that every candidate must be interviewed by five colleagues and be reference and salary checked before a job offer can be given to them. However, you interview a really outstanding candidate, who has only met one other colleague to date, and you realise this job seeker is about to accept a competitor's job offer. You decide to ignore the hiring rules and immediately extend her a written job offer.
- Your team have been working very well over a number of years with a supplier of a niche service. Under new procurement rules, you realize that this supplier should be dropped because they can't fulfil various compliance requirements but you decide to continue working with them, claiming that there's no other supplier in the market with their important skill-set.

Be wise

The secret is to be wise and sensible in deciding when and how you flout your company's written and unwritten rules. Never do so if it risks your career or reputation. If you have already overstepped the mark and made the mistake of ignoring a really important rule, seek the understanding and forgiveness of your boss or senior colleagues, and never do it again.

Be open and honest

When challenged, never deny having ignored a company policy. Calmly explain your rationale for not getting the right approvals, filling in the correct documentation or following a set timeframe.

Help change the rules if they're of no value

Be ready to speak up and suggest that a broken or useless policy is scrapped when it brings no value to the organization and perhaps is already being ignored by many colleagues without any negative impact.

Stay within the law

It should go without saying that breaking rules should never extend as far as breaking a particular country's laws.

- You might fire a member of your team without following all the requested internal procedures but never violate any applicable employment laws.
- Similarly, you might breach your company's expense limits when taking a client out for a celebration dinner but you must never give the client anything that might leave you accused of breaking an anti-bribery law in that country.

ACCEPT YOU MAY BE LONELY

'Leadership and loneliness often go hand in hand.'

It can be lonely as a leader and you must take care because this loneliness might be having a negative impact on your leadership performance. This was shown in a 2012 study conducted by the Harvard Business Review, which found that 50 per cent of CEOs said they experienced loneliness at work and, of these, 61 per cent felt it affected their performance.

This loneliness stems from having no one to open up to and share your troubles and concerns with. This is either because you may feel no one will understand what you're facing and going through or you feel it inappropriate to be open with certain people:

- Your staff may not understand and appreciate your leadership challenges
- You may have to keep many issues and decisions from your staff and this limits your ability to freely open up with them generally
- With your senior colleagues and with your own boss (if you have one), you may be reluctant to confide for fear of displaying vulnerability and weakness, which you fear they may use against you later.

This sense of being alone can be harder if you've been a member of the team you now manage. Before being promoted, you may have been very open and close with your colleagues but now you're the boss, they may treat you differently, for example, no longer inviting you to socialize.

You may also find that your busy schedule interferes with your social life and you have less free time to meet with family, friends and acquaintances. This can be very frustrating and can further exasperate any feelings of being alone as a leader.

Acknowledge your loneliness

Get used to the idea of being alone and not having a ready pool of colleagues to bounce ideas off, seek opinions from and to sense-check your thinking. Have the self-confidence to listen to yourself and to make some decisions on your own.

Make an alternative buddy or two

It may be possible to make some decisions alone but successful leaders pro-actively seek the counsel, support and advice of others when needed. They create an inner circle to support them. This may include:

- Reaching out to one or two trusted colleagues you have known for some time with whom you can confide and open up about your anxieties, concerns and fears. They may be individuals who are mentoring you as part of a programme.
- Befriending leaders working for other organizations, with whom you can open up, reflect, learn and brainstorm (without revealing confidential company information of course!). You could meet leaders at all kinds of networking events organized in your area by bodies such as Lions, Rotary, Chambers of Commerce, industry body associations and other private clubs (such as a local golf club).

Loneliness is not confined to leaders

In our technology driven world, many of us are feeling increasingly more isolated as we rely more on emails, messages and online video conferencing and less on physical face-to-face interactions. As well as monitoring your own feelings of loneliness, always keep an eye open for members of your own team who may be feeling lonely and disconnected, perhaps offering to spend time with them over a coffee or lunch.

MAKE THE RIGHT CALLS

'Your leadership journey will be made or broken by your key decisions and choices.'

Decision-making is such an important skill because, as a leader, your decisions could make or break your company's future as well as your own career.

Sadly, there's no magic recipe to ensure that every single decision you ever make will be perfectly baked. As you follow and read about leaders at some of the world's most successful companies such as Apple, Facebook, Alibaba, Samsung, Airbnb and Zara, you'll quickly learn that they have made some amazingly wise decisions along with some very poor ones. Sometimes the effect of a poor decision may only be visible to a few people internally, but sometimes poor leadership decisions can have such a large impact that their organization can make the world news:

- During the 2007–08 financial crash, some of the world's largest banks faced bankruptcy while the investment bank Lehman Brothers closed down.
- The Deepwater Horizon oil spill in 2010 cost British Petroleum its reputation and billions in compensation payments.
- In 2019, Boeing had to set aside a few billion dollars for compensation payments in the wake of the grounding of all 737 Max aircraft.
- Previously renowned global brands such as Blockbuster, Kodak, Toys R Us and Borders are all no longer trading.

Even if you only work in a small organization where the potential financial impact of a poor decision is only a few thousand dollars, you still need to avoid making mistakes like this if you want to be viewed as a successful leader and keep your job. The secret is to become expert at making decisions and minimize the risk of ever making one that might destroy your company or career.

Involve the right people

Never struggle alone with a challenging decision – always involve other people. Seek the help of whoever is most skilled within your team, colleagues, other stakeholders and experts. Ask them to evaluate and challenge you on your own understanding, thinking and assumptions. It's always better to have some really difficult discussions and arguments before eventually making the right decision than to quickly make a decision which proves to be wrong.

Use the right (decision-making) tools

Work with your team to always gather and analyse all aspects of a decision including the relevant facts, assumptions, risks and impacts. Learn about and appropriately use decision-making frameworks, models and processes. Your colleagues might be able to teach you how to use some of the better-known and relatively easy to understand ones such as:

- SWOT and PEST analyses
- Opportunity cost calculations
- Cost-benefit and weighted scoring analyses
- Decision trees and matrices
- Cause and effect fishbone diagrams
- Payback and Net Present Value (NPV) calculations.

What's the worst that could happen?

Never make a decision until you understand the potential negative impacts of that decision. Ask yourself whether your organization can cope in the event of a worse-case outcome.

Sometimes you'll discover that the potential risks of a decision are greater than the benefits. In such cases, have the humility and courage to consider altering or cancelling a planned decision. Better a little loss of face today than finding yourself fired later for making a decision that proved too costly.

PLAY PEACEMAKER

'Your leadership is only really tested when storm clouds gather and the seas become rough.'

Whenever people work together, you'll rarely have harmony and alignment with everyone in harmonious agreement about everything. Instead, there will always be moments of tension, arguments and conflicts within any team or organization. For example:

- Misunderstandings about what has been said or done by someone
- Tensions between colleagues as they fight over the same time slots, attention or resources
- Department heads accusing one another of lying about who agreed to take responsibility for solving an issue
- Disagreements over how to tackle a problem or achieve a goal
- Team members' egos clashing over who has the superior idea and should lead a discussion
- Jealousy over who received recognition for a completed project
- Colleagues who are not on speaking terms after someone took offence at comments made about them
- The boss breaking a promise to promote one of the team and promoting someone else instead, causing the slighted team member to become angry.

How you respond in such scenarios is a measure of your leadership maturity and wisdom. Too many leaders make problems worse by being part of the conflict themselves or jumping in and taking sides, or by being unaware of the issue at all or choosing to avoid it. By inflaming any conflict, a leader can turn even small matters into conflicts which then have devastating impacts on a team's productivity, collaboration and motivation. Successful leaders do the opposite – they never choose to create conflicts or to worsen conflicts that have already arisen if they can possibly avoid it.

Sniff out potential conflict

Always be on the lookout for situations where upset, arguments, misunderstandings or disagreements might emerge. When you sense a problem might be brewing, bring the affected individuals together and have frank discussions. Ask the sparring parties to:

- Remember their collective purpose, vision, goals and successes rather than only focusing on any potential areas of difference
- Continually talk together, working through any differences as soon as they arise, with you remaining as a mediator if needed.

Tackle fires already burning

When conflict has already started, be quick to eliminate any unhealthy emotions and feelings and help resolve the issue through encouraging all parties to:

- Pause and share their feelings, upset and concerns with you in confidence. Then bring all parties together in the same room (or through video conference), allowing all sides to hear one another's views and perceptions.
- Steer this conversation as needed to make sure that all needed opinions are aired, and that no one stays quiet when you know they have something to say.
- Find common ground and seek a compromise acceptable to all sides.

During these discussions, vary your leadership style as needed from very firm and directive through to stepping back and allowing the parties involved to find their own consensus and way forward, if that looks like it may produce results.

Allow healthy conflicts

Sometimes colleagues need to air differences and have moments of disagreement. All successful organizations recognize this and have a culture of healthy and productive disagreement. Just be sure to follow the advice on this page to stop these discussions turning into negative, tense and emotionally charged conflicts.

SPELL OUT RESPONSIBILITY

'An excellent leader never acts like a Teflon-coated non-stick frying pan.'

You can always spot a weak leader by how skilfully and quickly they're able to pin the blame on other people when challenged about mistakes, misunderstandings, missed targets and other poor performance-related issues. Such people can become expert at washing their hands of responsibility and accountability even when it's obvious to others that they're the person in charge of the relevant tasks and goals. You'll never succeed by acting in this way and will eventually be called out for shirking your responsibilities as a leader. You may even be fired as a result.

Successful leadership is about making things happen, implementing changes and achieving goals. To do these things, you must be systematic in allocating and assigning responsibility, including to yourself, to make sure that everybody understands exactly who is:

- Responsible for an actual task or piece of work – this could be one individual or a group and might include the leader.
- Accountable for the completion of that work – as a leader, you're probably the one who is ultimately answerable and responsible in this way. As you become more senior, leaders beneath you will be accountable for their own team's work but you may remain ultimately accountable.
- Asked to Support and/or be Consulted to help in the task's completion – they're normally only responsible for the quality of their help and advice.
- Needing to be kept Informed of the work and would normally have no responsibility.

Known as the RASCI model, this framework makes it easier for any leader and their team members to understand, accept and focus on the tasks and goals they're responsible and accountable for.

Advertise who is responsible

- Create your own version of the RASCI model, turning it into a table that lists the names of those who are solely or jointly responsible as well as accountable for different tasks and pieces of work.
- Have discussions and brainstorming sessions if needed to reach agreement on who is responsible and accountable for which tasks and goals.
- Support, motivate and encourage team members to take personal responsibility and/or accountability. If needed, be directive and forceful in allocating who does what.
- Be very clear about any shared responsibilities and ensure that those who are jointly responsible, including yourself, are aligned and able to work collaboratively.

Be the role model

Be a good role model by being enthusiastic and motivated to take full accountability for all of your team's work as well as for any tasks that you personally undertake.

Demonstrate that your team's failures are also your own

Never make the mistake of passing tasks to your team and later blaming them for poor performance or mistakes and thinking that you're absolved of any blame. You always remain accountable for your team's work – this is a fundamental role of leadership. Challenge and support them to complete the work themselves but never wash your hands when they struggle or fail.

BE ENTREPRENEURIAL

'Would you do the same thing if it were your own business?'

When you're a leader working for a business that is not your own, you can make decisions without needing to face the full consequences of the decisions' outcomes. The worst that could happen is you make bad decisions and get fired. However, when you're the entrepreneur who owns the business, a few poorly thought through decisions could leave you penniless if your firm goes bankrupt and your shareholding becomes worthless.

Entrepreneurs know that every decision they make has very high risks compared to a leader employed by a large corporation who is simply spending or investing the company's money. For this reason, successful entrepreneurs have some valuable skills and attributes that you should learn from:

- They're deeply thoughtful about choices and decisions facing them, given that their own money is always on the line
- They have honed their intuition and gut feelings to complement their analytical and intellectual skills to give them an extra edge
- They have a strong passion for the businesses they create, making them very inspiring, energetic and charismatic leaders
- They're extremely creative, love thinking out of the box and always taking the initiative in search of great ideas and solutions
- They're very good at motivating and encouraging others to join them on their start-up journeys.

You may never wish to put your capital on the line by becoming an entrepreneur, but emulating some of their success traits can raise your game.

Think and act like an entrepreneur

Whenever you're facing a problem, dilemma or decision and not sure which option to choose, ask yourself, 'Which would I choose if this were my own company and it were my own money on the line?' Having this owner's mindset gives you a heightened awareness and may cause you to think twice about a decision when most other leaders might think it through too quickly or even avoid dealing with it all together. With an entrepreneurial mindset, you might:

- Wonder if an underperforming employee should be terminated now rather than keeping them on and paying their salary in the hope that they will improve
- Double-check if the forecasted returns in a capital expenditure plan are really achievable or if your staff are being overly optimistic in their calculations
- Evaluate whether a long-term supplier is becoming complacent and not bringing the value-add they had promised and ask your team to seek more cost-effective alternatives.

In addition to being more thoughtful, two other entrepreneurial qualities to adopt are:

- Being passionate and enthusiastic about your goals, plans and workload, and viewing your job responsibilities as something you're choosing to do as if you were your own boss
- Becoming excited about wanting to improve and optimize all aspects of your work and business by bringing your intuition, creativity and innovation to everything you do.

Encourage others to think like entrepreneurs

When you start acting more entrepreneurial, your team may like your new-found passion and excitement. Equally, they may be surprised that you're acting more cautiously and probing every decision, forecast and plan they present to you. Explain why you're acting in this way and encourage them to also adopt an owner mentality when making their own decisions.

THINK GLOBALLY

'No leader succeeds as an island, cut off from the rest of the world.'

The world is so interconnected, with virtually every aspect of life and business becoming more global each year. It's now impossible to be a leader living and working in one city, county or region and ignore the rest of the world. The *New York Times* writer Thomas Friedman introduced this idea in his aptly titled book, *The World is Flat*, and today every part of a business seems to have links to other parts of the world:

- European High Street clothing brands selling clothes designed in Italy, made in Bangladesh with fabric from China, zippers from Japan and buttons from India
- US Companies having their call centres and back office support services located in places as far afield as India, Mexico or the Philippines serving staff and fielding calls from clients located in every corner of the world
- Sitting in your living room in Manchester or Chicago and purchasing almost anything from anywhere thanks to a multitude of global websites
- Supermarket shelves in any city stocked with products from every imaginable country
- When you take a look at any individual products, you discover just how global they are. To take one example – Airbus aircraft are assembled in France but with parts produced in many countries including the wings constructed in Wales in the UK.

Successful leaders understand just how global even the most local marketplace or business is becoming and actively seek to learn about and take advantage of this globalization.

Lead locally, think globally

Not everyone wants to become a global leader running a business spanning the world. You can be equally successful by leading a business which focuses on serving just one area or community with some great relationships with your local clients, suppliers and staff. But your local business, based in Edinburgh, Detroit or Toronto, risks missing out on so many great ideas and opportunities if you close your eyes to what is happening elsewhere.

If you're not doing so already, take a more global perspective starting with these small steps:

- Attend trade shows and expos that cover your industry sector, and that take place both within your country as well as overseas, to learn about what your local and global competitors are doing and about how products and services are evolving
- Consider sourcing materials, products and services from new locations
- Find a distributor or reseller in an overseas market to test how appealing and valuable having foreign customers may be
- Market and sell your products and services online to a global marketplace
- Be open to hiring staff with experience of working and living in other parts of the world.
- Read widely both about your industry as well as more broadly about global business trends and ideas.

Decide to network globally

Become involved in international business networking and referral networks such as BNI (www.bni.com) or the Entrepreneurs' Organization (www.eonetwork.org). You'll learn so much from spending time with leaders from all corners of the globe who will bring with them different insights, as well as giving you a network of new business friends who could support and aid any of your own international sourcing or expansion plans.

COPE WITH THE UNEXPECTED

'Sometimes leaders must twist and turn like snakes to cope with the unexpected.'

The best laid plans so often go up in smoke, don't they? As a leader, you need to skillfully cope with the consequences of any unexpected changes:

- A key member of your team who was your planned successor suddenly resigns leaving you with a massive workload and the headache of finding his replacement
- Your boss becomes seriously ill and you must cover for her while also temporarily reporting to a senior colleague who you don't know at all
- You team informs you that your largest client is taking their business to a cheaper supplier, leaving a large hole in your sales budget
- Your laptop crashes while starting a presentation at a global management meeting and you must continue without your slideshow and videos
- At the eleventh hour, you're asked to rework your department's budget numbers by incorporating a 10 per cent cost reduction.

Faced with all kinds of unexpected changes, too many leaders panic and become stressed, start complaining and moaning. Worst of all, they may even ignore what has happened and act as if nothing has changed.

Successful leaders, on the other hand, have mastered how to be successful even when their best laid plans go up in smoke. You need to learn how to emulate them when your own plans get messed up. They tend to exhibit a mix of being flexible, agile, resilient and mentally strong, and are quick to understand and process the changes in real-time and then calmly adjust their plans accordingly to ensure the best possible outcome.

Become adaptive and agile

Unexpected events must never stop you in your tracks and cause you to stop or give up. When faced with a roadblock, delay or unexpected event, follow these four suggestions:

1. Observe yourself and keep any emotional reactions, feelings of disappointment and upset in check.
2. Positively focus on the problem at hand, deciding quickly whether you must make any immediate changes or whether you have more time to react. Either way, respond optimally to the unexpected event, news or setback.
3. Explore the available information and decide whether you need to reprioritize what must be done and write a plan of action with clear timeframes.
4. Implement and communicate any necessary changes with a positive frame of mind, refocusing your time and attention as needed to ensure things quickly get back on track.

Bring your team with you

- Don't allow your team to become entrenched in what they're doing and unwilling to adjust and change as needed.
- Involve them in both understanding what has happened as well as in crafting a response.
- People are not stupid. Never feel that you must hide any bad news from them or leave them in the dark about how they will need to adapt.
- Give them extra care and attention – this will help them cope with whatever unexpected changes occur.

PEER INTO THE FUTURE

'Yesterday and today are poor predictors of what will land on you tomorrow.'

Successful leaders are futurists who always make time to look beyond what is happening today to peer into the future. They're like chess grandmasters who have honed their skills and foresight to be able to visualize many possible moves ahead in their chess games.

Looking into the future is no longer an optional activity for any leader, but has become an essential leadership task because of the world constantly being in flux. How the world you're leading in will appear in only a few years' time could be very different from today thanks to the numerous technology-driven changes impacting our already volatile, uncertain, complex and ambiguous (VUCA) world. Your very survival as a leader will depend on your foresight and strategic acumen, and your ability to adjust your vision and goals as needed. There are three key and interlocking areas you must keep an eye on:

1. Ensure that your company and its products and services will still be relevant and valued in the years ahead by evolving existing, and creating new, offerings to meet your changing market needs.
2. Understand and be ready to take advantage of trends in technology, talent, regulations and ways of working to make sure that your business' systems, procedures and use of resources remain optimal and best practice.
3. Help both yourself and your team members to discover and understand what skills, mindsets, education and work experiences need to be refreshed to keep you valuable and sought after as leaders and employees.

Find out where to learn

- Read online articles and studies at sites such as http://www.futurist.com and https://foresightprojects.blog.gov.uk, which explore future trends and possible scenarios effecting different industries and aspects of working life.
- Regularly attend conferences and expos that are relevant to the business sector you work within and/or your area of work expertise and interests.
- Explore online or in-person training courses that focus on topics such as the future of work or the future impact of technologies on the workplace. You could also seek out those targeted at your industry, business sector or job function such as a course on the future of financial services or those related to manufacturing. Many courses are available online as free MOOCs at sites such as www.futurelearn.com, www.edx.org or www.udemy.com.
- You could also explore becoming officially trained and certified in how to explore the future with organizations such as The Futurist Institute (www.futuristinstitute.org) and Global Foresight (www.globalforesight.org).

A word of caution – never blindly believe everything you hear or read because no one can predict the future with anything close to 100 per cent accuracy. Simply take on board the ideas and insights you hear to help you form your own evolving knowledge, insights, views, feelings and opinions.

Organize reflective brainstorming sessions

- Get involved in updating and reviewing your organization's vision, future direction and strategic plans.
- Help your team to regularly brainstorm what skills, knowledge and experiences they need in order to stay relevant and employable.
- Encourage your HR colleagues to source or organize training courses on skills that will be key for your team in the future.
- Stay on top of any changing leadership expectations and issues.

CHOOSE YOUR ROLE MODELS CAREFULLY

'Observe those who inspire and impress you, then emulate their positive qualities, but those only. No one is perfect.'

Many leaders have been blindly learning from the wrong role models simply because they emulate and copy other leaders without realizing they're doing it. This pattern of unconscious mimicking starts in our childhoods when we instinctively copy our parents. We take this same habit into adulthood. You can see this happening when people are meeting together and one person crosses their arms or legs and other people do the same thing without even realizing it. It's also likely that your first few close colleagues and bosses became your unconscious role models because you had no one else to observe and learn from.

Successful leaders stop relying upon this unconscious and automatic mimicking of those they work for or look up to, and deliberately choose their role models. In addition, once they have chosen a role model, they never copy all aspects of that leader's style because no leader is perfect. Instead, they only emulate the positive behaviours and habits while avoiding their role model's weaknesses:

- A highly visionary leader might also have an anger management problem and a low tolerance for certain people or behaviours
- A leader who has amazing decision-making skills when it comes to choosing successful business opportunities but may lack the skills to develop and grow a high-performing team
- A leader who always exceeds expectations by pushing staff to achieve their KPIs may have no idea about how to listen, inspire and coach people.

Choose role models wisely

Decide which leaders have qualities you would like to emulate and learn from, and which leaders you would never want to emulate or copy in a million years. The latter are known as negative role models – you can learn important lessons from them in terms of how not to be a leader.

If you're not sure who your desired role models are, take your time to find out by reading about and listening to all kinds of leaders through books, articles, podcasts, at events and/or in-person within your own organization. Do you prefer to learn, for example, from successful leaders with similar backgrounds or experiences to your own, such as being a man or woman, or from a particular ethnic, work or educational background?

Do change your role models over time in alignment with your own growth as a leader. The ideal role models for you when you lead a small sales or software team will be quite different to those you need when you're appointed Managing Director of an entire company.

Maximize what you learn from role models

- Read their biographies and other material they have written
- If a role model is a colleague or family friend, you have hit the jackpot because you can easily meet them in person and even ask them whether they would be willing to coach or mentor you
- If your role models are far away or you don't know them personally, consider connecting with them (via linkedin.com) to ask them specific questions
- Keep a journal of your notes and reflections about what you learn from your role models and about your own attempts to emulate some of their better habits and behaviours while avoiding the bad ones.

GET OFF YOUR HIGH HORSE

'Nelson Mandela left us with one key learning – always forgive people even when it seems impossible to do.'

Most people are unforgiving and refuse to forgive a colleague who has done something to upset them. Too many leaders act the same and are unwilling to let it go, reconcile and move on. They prefer instead to hold onto their negative feelings and tell people how they have been wronged.

The problem with not forgiving someone is that *you* suffer – not other person. You're the one holding onto the negative feelings towards them and the resentment you hold onto might turn you into an over-critical, bitter and negative leader. Not surprisingly, being the opposite – a forgiving leader – can help you both to lead as well as to create a better working environment. In a 2017 study reported in the *Journal of Management and Organization*, the authors concluded that being a forgiving leader helps you and your team interact and collaborate more optimally. This makes sense and I have observed this in my coaching work, finding that leaders who are more forgiving:

- Enable people to take more risks, make mistakes and to speak up
- Help those they work with to become more understanding and forgiving
- Create a more motivating, compassionate and positive work environment.

Successful leaders understand all of these benefits and always make an effort to forgive other people as well as themselves. They don't forget what has happened but choose to no longer carry the negative feelings inside themselves and instead make a conscious decision to move on.

Understand how unforgiving you're being

Recognize when you're being unwilling to forgive other people. Discover your patterns, reflect upon them and observe when you're:

- Holding a grudge or retaliating against someone
- Feeling mistreated, ignored or hurt by someone
- Writing someone off for making a mistake
- Angry about someone doing something
- Teaching someone a lesson by refusing to make-up after an argument
- Refusing to accept another person's apologies and contrition
- Ignoring someone's attempts to make good on something they had said or done.

...and work to become genuinely forgiving

- Decide whether you really want to become a more forgiving person. If you have a large ego, it may take extra effort to forgive, let go and move on. When you feel torn between holding firm and being forgiving, do speak to a close colleague who could help you see sense and help you to forgive.
- Decide whether you want to write a note or email to explain your perceptions and feelings and/or to meet the other person face to face in your office, a meeting room or over lunch.
- Your forgiveness won't change the past nor make it disappear but it will allow you and your colleagues to optimally move forward together without holding onto any excess and negative baggage.
- People are rarely 100 per cent in the right and your challenge may not just be about forgiving someone else but also about you saying sorry and apologizing for your part in an argument, misunderstanding or for how you reacted.

...and remember to forgive yourself

Remember that you may also need to forgive yourself and to stop beating yourself up for things you may have done wrong in the past.

STAND TALL DURING STORMS

'Never lose your composure and focus even when living through a Force 10 Hurricane.'

If you haven't already, you'll face all kinds of crises during your time as a leader that can impact profit targets, project plans, careers, reputations or even peoples' livelihoods and lives. How you react and lead during these critical moments can make or break your leadership career. You need to be ready to tackle any crisis really well, no matter how it occurred:

Caused by events that are out of your control	Caused by events that are within your control
• Freak weather causing your electronics factory to be flooded and stopping production indefinitely • Economic sanctions imposed on your main export market resulting in your sales revenue falling 25%	• A deadly fire at your chemicals plant caused by old wiring and paper rubbish which you knew about • A poorly tested new product explodes when used by customers, resulting in a global product recall

Your leadership nightmare is facing a crisis that you could have contained but allowed to grow or even spiral out of control because you overreacted, made poor decisions or failed to understand and listen well. A worse mistake is to try to hide or downplay a crisis because you know your organization is at fault. We see many examples of this withholding of the truth:

- An oil company is slow to reveal that a major offshore oil leak is happening because they know it's their fault and their delay in coming clean creates an even larger environmental disaster with a bigger financial cost to them.
- An airline manufacturer is reluctant to admit that one of its aircraft models is flying with a potentially catastrophic technical problem which they knew about, and their delay worsens the bad publicity and financial impact.

Successful leaders avoid these leadership mistakes and, instead, practise high-quality crisis management to minimize the negative impacts of any possible problem.

Master key crisis management skills

It's essential that your responses to and actions during a crisis won't worsen an already difficult situation for you and your colleagues.

Be calm, honest and open

Remain steady and balanced even when those around you might be panicking, crying, acting fearful or anxious. When you need to calm yourself, sit down, close your eyes and take slow deep breaths. Pause before saying or doing anything to be sure that your message or action will be helpful and is not simply a knee-jerk reaction to the problem or you being defensive and hiding something.

Evaluate and act decisively

Create a crisis management team made up of colleagues with differing skill-sets and experiences who together make a strong team to help solve the issue. Work together to evaluate what is happening and understand the reasons for the problem. Decide what urgent short-term actions need to happen now such as writing an initial press release, informing the company's shareholders or providing emergency assistance to those affected.

Treat the crisis with the same seriousness you would give to an important work project – detailed planning, agreeing which stakeholders to involve and identifying the necessary actions, resources, timeframes and communications.

Keep appropriate stakeholders informed

There will be different people involved in each problem, each having their own perceptions of the crisis and expectations of how it can be solved. Regularly communicate with all parties, keeping them informed and never lie to them, hold back information or keep quiet. Share with your team and colleagues your plans and commitments, including your vision of how you'll lead the team or organization through the crisis and beyond.

VALUE DIVERSITY AND INCLUSIVITY

'We discriminate against certain people without even noticing.'

Diversity is a hot topic. In today's working world we are all very well informed, trained and supported to never knowingly discriminate, show any bias or to treat anyone differently because of who they are. We are encouraged to create gender balanced teams, give everyone equal opportunities and to hire and to promote those from disadvantaged and under-represented backgrounds.

You might be proud of how you're always conscious of diversity issues but most of your decisions and choices are actually being made by your unconscious mind. The Nobel-winning scientist Eric Kandel believes that nearly all of our thinking is hidden away from us in this way.

This wouldn't be a problem if our unconscious minds were always making great choices and decisions for us. But sadly, a lot of the time, our brains are making biased split-second assessments and judgements of people and situations, influenced by our backgrounds, personal experiences, cultures and what makes us more comfortable. Thanks to this biased thinking, we all exhibit what is called unconscious bias:

- We are drawn to people who look, act and sound like us, while also tending to view people who are taller and fitter as having more authority and deserving more respect
- We favour job candidates from certain academic and work backgrounds that fit with our own
- During meetings, women are often ignored, spoken over and their comments not valued compared to those of men
- When a woman acts like a man, she can be accused of being too aggressive, whereas when a man acts in the same way he might be viewed as exhibiting an excellent leadership style
- We are influenced by a person's name and are drawn to those we are more familiar with. This is why some companies remove candidates' names from their CVs before sharing with interviewers.

To perform more successfully as a leader, it's time you stopped making such unconscious choices, which can be unhelpful and are often totally unacceptable.

Understand how you're biased

Start by understanding and acknowledging when you might be guilty of unconscious bias:

- Take the well-known Implicit Association Test from Harvard University. It's free to take and is available online at https://implicit.harvard.edu/implicit/iatdetails.html. It shows which of your individual perceptions and actions are being determined by your unconscious biases.
- Observe yourself, noting when you might be automatically jumping to conclusions or assumptions about different people you're interacting with.

Open up and consciously diversify your thinking

- When in situations where your biases might be evident, pause and ask yourself honest questions such as 'Am I really preferring this job candidate because of her work experience or just because she also went to the same University as I did?'
- When you meet someone for the first time, ask yourself what your first impressions are and reflect on which of your biases might have helped determine your answer. Decide whether this is a fair conclusion to make. Do you need to be more open-minded?
- Always try to broaden your focus, for example by ensuring that women attending your meetings are not spoken over or ignored.
- Encourage your colleagues to also understand what unconscious bias is and why it's so bad if we blindly allow it to make our decisions for us.
- Read about the different types of biases that you may be guilty of having.

LEAD WITH YOUR BODY LANGUAGE

'Stand tall, smile and show that you're ready to lead.'

Your non-verbal communication is at least as important as your verbal. As a result, it doesn't matter how brilliant your choice of words is – if your body language is telling your audience a different story, don't be surprised if your message gets lost:

- You have written an inspiring speech to give in a town hall meeting, but it will fall on deaf ears if you slump your shoulders, wear ill-fitting clothes, stare at the floor, look sad or speak in a monotone.
- You're giving a well-designed interactive presentation to impress a potential new client, but this will mean nothing if your handshake is limp and weak, your shoelaces are untied, you mumble your words, keep your arms crossed and act nervous.

Excellent all-round communication skills are not just a nice-to-have skill, they are essential. As a leader, you're an ambassador – how people see and hear you has a disproportionately large impact on the success of your organization as well as upon your own leadership career. Successful leaders are conscious of the impact of all four aspects of their communication:

1. Verbal – what you say in terms of your choice of words
2. Para-verbal – how you say what you say, which includes your tone and volume of voice and intonation
3. Non-verbal – your facial expressions, eye contact and body posture
4. Appearance – your clothing, make-up and body odour.

Have your communication work for, not against you

Work on all four areas of your communication and invest the needed time and effort to strengthen/overcome whichever elements of how you communicate are helping you stand out and/or are holding you back:

Verbal

When you're preparing for an important talk or speech, prepare your words in advance and share them with someone who is a skilled wordsmith and willing to edit and improve your draft. Be equally thorough before any meetings by thinking through how you'll craft your arguments and make the necessary points.

Para-verbal

Make a constant effort to make sure that what you want to say is never weakened or over-shadowed by verbal distractions such as using too many filler words (such as *um* and *ah*), having long pauses, sighing, stuttering and inappropriate giggling.

Non-verbal

Have someone film you while you're giving a talk and then be honest. Is your non-verbal communication working for or against you? Practise overcoming typical mistakes such as having odd or unusual facial expressions and hand gestures, not standing upright in a calm and relaxed manner, appearing to look sad or not looking at people you're speaking with.

Appearance

Be well groomed, with neat hair and clean shoes. Wear clothes that you feel comfortable in as well as make you look very professional. Your choice of appearance is partly determined by your work environment. When you're unsure what to put on in the morning, remember the saying 'When in Rome do as the Romans do'. Dress like those you'll be interacting and working with.

LEAVE YOUR DOOR OPEN

'Great leaders never hide in their offices.'

To bring out the best in a team, a leader must be willing to listen to whatever the team members wish to communicate. Be careful though – this isn't as simple as leaving your office door physically open. I once coached a leader who claimed to be very approachable with her door literally wide open but her staff told me they hated speaking with her. They explained that whenever they approached her with ideas, problems or suggestions, she acted like she had no time, would make them feel unwelcome, or would ridicule and find fault in their ideas rather than saying anything positive.

Genuinely approachable leaders make their staff feel at ease, patiently listen, reflect and calmly respond without any judgement. This is a genuine open-door policy and helps create a very healthy and positive working environment:

- As a result of being heard, people will feel more valued and motivated and will be willing to invest more effort in their work.
- It creates a working culture of increased openness, trust and transparency in which people will be less inclined to remain silent and hold back from sharing with each other, including with you.
- There will be less fear and more eagerness to discuss problems and issues before they become fully fledged crises.

77

Have an open door policy (but with some boundaries)

Always aim to be ready and available to speak with your team members, but have them understand this does not mean you're always literally available every time a team member asks to speak with you. You might be busy finishing an urgent report, reflecting on a problem or deep in discussion with a client. When in this situation, be polite and explain that you're keen to talk as soon as possible and agree a time when you're both available to sit down. Be sure to block the time in your diary to avoid double booking yourself.

Don't dismiss your team's concerns and worries

Be considerate and kind when one your team brings up an issue which you might be tempted to dismiss as trivial, small or an overreaction. Hide this initial thought and listen to your staff to show that you value their contribution. You don't have to agree with them but at least hear them out. If you don't, they're likely to stop speaking up and sharing with you in the future.

Don't shoot the messenger

When a team member approaches you with some bad news, be careful to not overreact by showing your anger or that you're upset. Be grateful that they have told you something that others may have been keeping quiet about. Positively thank them for having the courage and good sense to bring up the issue, encouraging them to always speak up.

Don't wait for them to come to you

To demonstrate that you're truly accessible, don't wait for your team to approach you. Instead, be proactive and go and find them by regularly walking around your office or shop floor, stopping to talk with your staff and asking them how things are. Invite them to come to talk with you whenever they like.

BECOME CULTURALLY INTELLIGENT

'When you're working far from your home, YOU are the odd one out.'

In today's interconnected world, there are so many people working away from their own countries. It's highly likely you'll find yourself interacting and leading people from many different cultures and the potential to be misunderstood, cause offence or create confusion is quite high. What you view as normal and may do without thinking might be misunderstood by others and cause them to feel uncomfortable or even offended. Being ignorant about cultural differences or making fun of them could easily damage your business, reputation and career.

- President Obama once made a cultural blunder by greeting the Burmese leader Aung San Suu Kyi with a kiss on her cheek. This is a very taboo thing to do in Myanmar. If you had done the same thing, you could have lost an important Burmese business deal over your cultural faux pas.
- Your company's business dealings could have come to an abrupt halt in Mexico had you copied Jeremy Clarkson, who once made remarks that were so offensive about Mexicans that the Mexican Ambassador in London complained to the BBC about the 'outrageous, vulgar and inexcusable insults'.

Successful leaders have learnt to become culturally sensitive and to appreciate the many cultural differences that exist in how people:

- Greet, come close and touch each other
- Express that they agree or understand something
- Dress, dance, travel, eat and drink
- Speak up, complain, celebrate and share or remain quiet
- Are impacted by their religion and religious festivals
- Interact, work and socialize together
- Treat women and men differently
- Question and challenge each other
- Treat time and deadlines differently
- Make agreements and promises.

Learn about the cultures of your colleagues

- When you have a new colleague, client or supplier from another part of the world, do a little research on the customs, unwritten rules and practices of men and women from that country or area.
- Seek advice about the dos and don'ts by searching the web, using a phone app such as 'compare cultures' and by reading books on culture by experts such as Geert Hofstede, Richard D. Lewis and Erin Meyer.

If in doubt, ask and always apologize

- Ask those you're working or travelling with to share with you information about their own cultural norms, expectations and taboos.
- Invite them to share their own observations about your own culture, explaining what appears similar or different to their own.
- Encourage them to point out when you may be on the verge of doing something culturally inappropriate that may upset or embarrass people.
- Note, however, that in many cultures people are accustomed to being very polite and will never tell you that you have offended them. You may have to find out through your own research and by talking with as many people as possible.
- Always apologize, in a culturally appropriate manner, when you have caused offence.

THE CUSTOMER ALWAYS COMES FIRST

'Never forget the one who is ultimately paying the salaries of your entire team.'

Everything you do as a leader is linked to fulfilling your customers' needs. The impact might be direct if you're heading a sales team, or indirect if you and your team are supporting colleagues who are your internal clients. Only by fulfilling all their needs can you be sure of maintaining your company's success as well as your own. No matter whether you're the CEO or a new manager, you need to ensure that you and your team are always performing well so that your internal and external customers continually receive what they're expecting and paying for.

- You're the head of a finance team and must ensure that your team doesn't reimburse expenses incorrectly, pay salaries late or create invoices containing errors. Otherwise, you'll upset your internal and external customers.
- As an IT manager, you must make sure that all of your colleagues' technology requirements are being met and that key IT systems are never offline. If you don't, your company may not be able to serve its customers.
- You head a procurement team and the pricing, quality and timing of your team's purchases impacts the work of your colleagues in production and sales, which ultimately impacts the external customers' products.

Successful leaders understand this well, and will move mountains to ensure that external customers' needs and wishes are satisfied (or exceeded) so that their organization remains their valued partner and supplier.

Get to know your customers well

- Always make a conscious effort to spend time with your internal customers to fully understand their needs and expectations. Appreciate the importance and impact of your help and support, and understand the impact of when your team are slow or make mistakes.
- Be innovative and creative to unearth ways in which you can add extra value to what your internal customers need to create and produce.
- If your internal customers are in turn serving other internal customers, understand each part of this internal value chain or pipeline by also spending time in the departments or sections served by your internal customers.
- Understand your external customers and how they're using your company's products and services. No matter whether you work in finance, HR, marketing, production or internal audit, try to visit at least one key customer annually, and encourage your team members to do the same. Ask a salesperson to accompany you on one of their regular visits.

CHOOSE YOUR WORDS CAREFULLY

'Why are you crying? I am only trying to explain how you can do a better job next time.'

You can so easily get it wrong when speaking with colleagues. You may start out with the best of intentions but then your choice of words and speaking style comes across wrong and you end up demotivating, upsetting or even angering somebody:

- You want to help a colleague to better understand a problem she's facing and you're accused of intruding and sounding condescending.
- You're passionate about a new business solution that your company could provide but colleagues complain that you're becoming obsessed and too evangelical about the idea.
- In a meeting, you question a colleague about his idea, intending to help him fine-tune it, but he feels you're not trusting or valuing his contribution.
- You offer your reasoned critique of a team member's project update and afterwards she complains that you sounded upset and extremely critical.
- You ask a colleague a range of questions about why an important deadline has been pushed back and he accuses you of interrogating him.
- You only make very brief comments when reviewing a team member's work and she becomes angry, claiming that you're not interested in her work.
- You suggest to your team a number of ways in which they could avoid repeating a big mistake and, instead of hearing your advice, they feel you're patronizing them and treating them like a child.

If you have not yet realized it, people are very sensitive and always liable to jump to conclusions and to assume you have the worst of intentions. Make sure that what you want to say equates with what the other party actually hears, feels and perceives.

Know your intention and execute it accordingly

Before speaking with colleagues, think about your desired intention and the impact of what you want to say. Then plan how you'll communicate your message so that it's clearly understood without the other party misinterpreting. So, the next time you're planning to:

- **Point out an error or mistake** – avoid sounding too harsh, critical and personal when addressing those who may be at fault.
- **Describe or clarify something** – be careful not to speak for too long and risk boring everybody or saying so little that nobody can understand you.
- **Explore and better understand something** – be measured in the number and form of questions you ask someone to avoid sounding like an interrogator who is not trusting what they're being told.
- **Give someone feedback or opinion of their work** – if you only say a few words, they may think that you're uninterested or not respecting them.
- **Share alternative opinions and views** – if you do so too strongly or emphatically, they might think you're personally attacking a colleague, and not just challenging their opinion.

Ask what the other party is hearing and feeling

Observe yourself as you speak, pausing as soon as you realize that you may becoming too strong or extreme with your words. Ask the other party how they're feeling and apologize when you fear your style of conversation might be unintentionally overstepping the mark and causing upset:

- 'It isn't my intention to be critical or harsh and I do hope you're not beginning to feel upset.'
- 'I realize that I have been firing lots of questions at you and I hope you don't feel that I am interrogating or over-challenging you. I apologize if I gave you that impression.'

MOTIVATE TO RETAIN YOUR TALENT

'One poorly thought-through request or action can demotivate an entire team.'

It takes great skill to be a leader who is able to create and maintain a work environment where staff come to work each morning motivated and with a positive mindset. It takes effort maintaining a team's motivation because each of us can become upset and demotivated for any number of reasons:

- Losing out on a promotion we feel we deserve
- Being ignored by our boss who shows favouritism to other colleagues
- Failing to be given a salary increase despite being promised one
- Not being given the recognition for completing a project on time
- Working over the weekend without any compensation
- Spending time working under a negative and cold boss
- Finding that the work has become repetitive and monotonous.

The impact of having demotivated team members can be costly to you and your business:

- They may come to work but lack the interest and energy to fully contribute. They will take less initiative, no longer speak up, collaborate less and may behave negatively. Such behaviours are toxic and contagious, quickly turning a positive and productive working environment into an unhealthy one.
- They might resign and you must cope with both the loss of their knowledge and experience as well as needing to spend time finding, training and bringing their replacements up to speed.
- Your reputation might suffer if your demotivated staff give you low scores in any employee engagement survey or in your annual 360-degree feedback. In addition, in their exit interviews, your resigning staff may speak harshly of you and their departure will worsen your talent retention statistics.

Help your staff fulfil their basic needs

Each of us has seven basic needs which, if fulfilled, can leave us highly motivated and engaged. Your task as a leader is to ensure that what you say and do is always helping your team meet these needs:

1. **Need to be valued** – always acknowledge your staff and thank them for their work and contribution.
2. **Need to have variety** – your staff will rarely want to do the same monotonous work each day and will become easily bored. Whenever possible, give them variety such as giving them ad hoc tasks, project responsibilities, opportunities to travel or to swap their job roles with others.
3. **Need to grow** – invest your time in helping your staff to grow in terms of exposure, responsibilities, experience, skill-set and so on.
4. **Need to connect with others** – create a very collaborative work environment where staff are encouraged to interact, help and support each other. Support having social activities including team dinners, family outings and sports events.
5. **Need to contribute** – help your team understand how their work fits into the bigger picture of your company's purpose, vision, and goals.
6. **Need to have certainty** – your staff need to know what is happening and what they have to do, and will dislike the unexpected. Always communicate plans and openly share information about any upcoming changes.
7. **Need to leave a legacy** – help each of your team to find meaning in their work and to take pride in what they accomplish and create.

ALWAYS UNDERSTAND THE NUMBERS

'All leadership issues involve numbers in one way or another.'

Be careful if your financial knowledge is really basic and you want a long and successful leadership career. These two things are mutually exclusive because all leadership roles involve money in one way or another. Many of your leadership responsibilities will be finance-related and include:

- Cost centres to manage, which involve being responsible for a range of expenditures
- Financial budgets to create and to compare your department's or business's actual revenues, expenses and capital expenditures against
- Business and strategic plans to create and execute
- Agreeing pricing and other financial terms with your clients
- Financial investments to make in property, working capital and new product developments
- Financial accounts to be audited, which you may need to review, approve and/or sign off on
- Hiring new staff and agreeing their remuneration
- Signing up new suppliers and negotiating terms of any contracts.

You risk making poor decisions and mistakes if you don't understand the financial impacts and consequences of your actions. Successful leaders know this and build up enough financial knowledge to succeed in their roles and to avoid mistakes such as:

- Being financially cheated and taken advantage of by being overcharged for work provided or having your staff cheat on their expenses
- Agreeing badly calculated pricing with clients or suppliers that may result in financial losses for their company
- Signing off on budgets, forecasts and project plans that have key items missing.

Become financially literate

It's time for you to learn the basics of finance and accounting. Luckily, this can be easily achieved through a combination of:

- Taking one of the many free 'basics in finance' online courses often referred to as MOOCs
- Reading books focused on teaching finance to non-finance managers
- Attending a short finance course at a Business School or organized by an accounting certification body such as the UK's Chartered Institute of Management Accountants (CIMA) or the American Institute of Certified Public Accountants (AICPA)
- Ask your finance and accounting-focused colleagues to teach and mentor you, and ask them to help you understand your company's different financial reports and statements.

As a minimum, seek to understand:

- Profit and loss statements, balance sheets and cashflow statements
- Key ratios of profitability and capital employed
- Product costing, pricing and margin calculations
- Budgeting and forecasting, including how to compare actual versus forecast revenues, expenses and capital expenditure
- Bank funding and others sources of financing and debt.

If already an expert, look beyond the numbers

Perhaps you've studied finance and business at university, qualified as a financial analyst or accountant while working or have already learnt about finance and money earlier in your career. Don't fall into the trap of complacency by either taking your eye off the numbers or doing the opposite and only focusing only on them while ignoring the human impact of financial decisions you need to make.

Make time and offer to share your knowledge by teaching your non-financial colleagues the essentials of finance.

EMBRACE TECHNOLOGY

'Don't be a technology-fearing Luddite.'

New technologies fuelled by the internet and high-speed computing are having an effect on every aspect of your work and life as a leader and are very hard to ignore:

- Thanks to smartphones with apps such as WhatsApp and FaceTime, everybody is contactable 24/7 at no cost.
- With real-time data analytics, we can know and understand everything that is happening to our businesses as soon as it has occurred.
- With global social media platforms and analysis of users' behaviours, we can understand all our actual and potential consumers' preferences, tastes and needs.
- The online storage of business data including in the form of emails and transactions (between staff, suppliers and customers) creates an environment where everything is in the open and can be tracked and monitored.
- Evolving automated processes involving advanced software, robotics and Artificial Intelligence are changing every workplace, from offices and warehouses through to factories and retail outlets.

You'll fail as a leader if you hide away from technological changes either by not learning about them or being reluctant to try things out and experiment:

- Your competitors will be more tech savvy and will overtake your company
- Your business model will become slow and antiquated
- Your consumers will be better served by other suppliers
- Your staff will feel that their workplace is falling behind the times
- You'll lose career opportunities as colleagues start to view you as a dinosaur.

You have no choice – openly and positively embrace evolving technologies.

Embrace the cutting edge

Have the clear intention of wanting your organization, your team, as well as yourself, to benefit and gain in this world of fast-changing technologies.

- Constantly learn about technological innovations, solutions, services and products that may impact and/or be introduced into your organization.
- Read online articles, talk with technology-fluent colleagues and visit relevant conferences and expos. If you know of other companies that have already taken the plunge and adopted a particular technology, visit them too.
- Volunteer to be the first to explore and experiment with new ideas, such as when your company is looking for a department head or team leader to trial a new smartphone customer relationship management app, or try out an upgraded version of an online performance management tool.

Help your staff face tech disruptions positively

Be a leader who has an optimistic vision about the changes and disruptions brought by new technologies and encourage your team to be interested in new technologies and their impacts. Help them to understand that they must be ready to learn and adapt, and to view any changes as career opportunities.

Tough decisions will be necessary

Be prepared for some difficult decisions and actions, such as needing to lay off staff as a result of technology-fuelled changes to how the work gets done. Give these staff as much warning time, re-learning opportunities and job-hunting support as possible. If funds permit, you could arrange for them to be given the services of a career coaching or outplacement firm.

You also need to make an extra effort to motivate and engage your remaining team members, who'll be shaken by the loss of their colleagues. They may be wondering if and when it will be their turn to see their jobs become automated and phased out.

NEGOTIATE YOUR WAY TO SUCCESS

'Be prepared to negotiate with everyone you meet.'

A successful leader is a skilled negotiator, who must constantly use their negotiation skills to seek alignment and agreement with many different people for all kinds of reasons. Examples include:

- Staff over changes to their employee benefits and other proposed changes
- Clients over pricing disagreements or product quality issues
- Suppliers over differing delivery dates
- A team to agree how a new process is to be implemented.

The benefits of being a successful negotiator who is able to reach agreement and alignment with other people can be substantial. These include:

- Avoiding tense conflicts and arguments that could cause you to fall out with a client, government department, supplier, shareholder or employee
- Eliminating wasted time and energy spent in waiting, misunderstanding and arguing
- Being able to implement plans, ideas and goals
- Creating higher levels of synergy, trust and engagement, which over time can improve client satisfaction, employee retention and engagement and business performance.

Given these benefits, it's no surprise that negotiation skills training is often mandatory for leaders. In my coaching and mentoring work, helping leaders to hone their negotiation skills is a common request.

Practise these key negotiation skills

- **Know your own position**

Before communicating with the other party, identify what you wish to achieve, what the range of acceptable outcomes is for you and how flexible you are able and willing to be. Have relevant information to hand to help you explain your arguments, suggestions and points of view, and also to help understand the other side's position.

- **Acknowledge differences**

Sometimes it may not be clear to the other person that there's an issue needing to be resolved. It can be very helpful to clearly spell it out, explaining your understanding of the issue at hand.

- **Listen to the other party**

Before you start proposing your solutions, ask the other side to share what they understand, observe, and hope to achieve. Actively listen to them, thank them for being open and acknowledge where you're in agreement.

- **Keep discussions and communications healthy**

Agree with the other side how you'll discuss and resolve your issue. Try to make it more personal by speaking together face to face rather than relying upon emails or lawyers' letters. Make an effort to build rapport and trust through being as honest and open together as you possibly can.

- **Be willing to walk away**

If you're not able to reach an acceptable agreement (or so-called negotiated settlement), decide whether to stop trying to negotiate and simply walk away. If you are willing and able to walk away, determine what the next best outcome is. This is sometimes referred to as the 'best alternative to a negotiated agreement' (BATNA). As an example, if you're trying to hire someone into your team and you fail, your BATNA might be to promote an internal colleague or to second another candidate from a sister company.

RESIGN FOR YOUR BELIEFS... IF NECESSARY

'Better to fail because of what you believe in than succeed at things you don't.'

Never make the common mistake of staying on in a leadership position when you're repeatedly forced to act in ways that go against your beliefs, ethics or integrity.

You may not know what is important to you until the day you find yourself in a situation where you feel uncomfortable and know something is wrong. This might be when you're expected to play along with your colleagues in:

- Deceiving customers by downplaying the health risks of the products that your company produces
- Pretending that your products contain 100 per cent recycled and biodegradable packaging
- Repeatedly promising staff salary increases and improved working conditions when you know this won't happen
- Lying to your auditors about your company's actual invoiced revenues or balance sheet accruals
- Covering up cases of sexual harassment or racial discrimination occurring within your company.

When faced with these kinds of issues, far too many leaders keep quiet, saying things such as:

- 'If I speak up, I will come under peer pressure to shut up and may even be fired.'
- 'If I leave, people will wonder why I resigned and I may struggle to find a new role.'
- 'Maybe I am being too demanding and the issue is not so serious after all.'
- 'I can't rock the boat as I need the salary to pay my mortgage and school fees.'
- 'All organizations face similar issues so I may as well stay here.'

Successful leaders never act in this way, closing one eye to what is happening. They find the courage to speak up and may even resign and move on. For them, whenever their beliefs and ethics are at odds with those of their senior bosses and colleagues, they will never allow fears or job security to allow them to compromise their convictions.

Open up and seek advice

When confronted with an issue at work that is challenging your convictions, speak up and talk about it with someone you trust. Try to open up with someone who is not working in the same company to avoid the possibility that they might share your concerns with other colleagues, which would cause you embarrassment.

Ask them whether they think you're being reasonable in feeling the way you do about a particular issue. Explore with them how you'll respond in terms of:

- Keeping quiet or speaking up
- Staying on in your role or resigning.

Become a whistleblower

If your company has a whistleblowing programme where you're able to anonymously bring up issues, you could follow this route to raise your concern about a particular business practice. If this proves futile because your CEO, senior colleagues and/or board of directors don't act upon your tip off and even try to suppress it, you could choose to talk about the issue with an industry watchdog, ombudsman or regulatory authority. Failing that, you could contact the media.

Protect yourself by taking legal advice given the high likelihood that in your employment contract you'll have agreed to some very clear and all-encompassing confidentiality and non-disclosure clauses.

Find a new leadership role before resigning

If you sense that you may end up resigning over some kind of unacceptable business and ethical practices, try to plan ahead by finding a new job before you tender your resignation.

SMASH THROUGH CEILINGS

'Never allow others to hold you back just because of who or what you are.'

A whopping 25 per cent of UK employees have experienced workplace discrimination, according to two 2018 surveys, one by Sky plc and the other by Learnlight. In the US, a 2017 study found that 42 per cent of women have faced workplace discrimination while another 2017 study discovered that over half of African Americans have faced discrimination in terms of pay and promotions.

In chapter 75, I encouraged you to be a leader who is never biased towards other people, but what happens when you're personally faced with other people's unconscious bias, or even outright discrimination, against you – discrimination that could risk derailing your leadership career and success? When in a junior job role, you might want to ignore such things, trying not to rock the boat or claiming that it's a one-off. But once in a leadership position, the discrimination may become more obvious and pronounced and it may be impossible to ignore its effects, for example:

- Being passed over for promotion into a more senior leadership role
- Not being entrusted with leading a high-profile project
- Being paid less than other leaders performing similar roles
- Failing to be shortlisted and interviewed for a leadership position in another company
- Not being respected and treated as a leader by your colleagues and/or bosses.

Value yourself

Be yourself and never hide any aspect of yourself, while always trying to break through any barriers that may be holding back your career. Allow your strengths to come through in your work performance and interactions with colleagues.

When you face any type of discrimination or bias, calmly investigate, speak up and talk about it. Ask the others involved to understand, apologize and change. If your bosses and colleagues treat you unequally, challenge them by discussing it. If they don't respond in a fair and authentic way, consider resigning and seeking a healthier working environment.

In my coaching work, the areas in which leaders typically feel discriminated unfairly against are regarding remuneration and performance ratings:

- If you feel are you being underpaid based on some aspect of your background, speak with your boss and HR colleagues to seek clarification. Push for remuneration comparable to what leaders in similar roles to yours are earning.
- If you receive a lower than expected performance rating and evaluation, don't rush to assume it's because of bias or discrimination. It may be. But it could also be a correct rating and you might be accused of trying to divert attention away from actually being an under-performing leader.

Help others break through their own glass ceilings

If you're a leader who is female, from a particular ethnic group, religion or socio-economic background, or a member of the LGBT community, be a role model. Give lunchtime talks, be a mentor or write in your in-house magazine and openly share about your own career journey and struggles to succeed in spite of being too old, female, Asian, transgender and so on. This may well encourage other colleagues to speak up about their own career ambitions being thwarted by various kinds of bias and of having had to jump through more hoops to arrive at where they are today.

DON'T IGNORE THAT ELEPHANT IN THE ROOM

'If you leave the elephant unattended, you might return to find all your furniture is destroyed.'

Far too many organizations and work environments have problems and issues that are not being addressed. This is often due to people being unwilling to rock the boat, upset people or become immersed in tricky, sensitive issues. Left undiscussed, such issues then fester and grow, which can damage your business' performance, working culture, staff morale and even your own credibility. Examples of such elephants in the room include:

- Everyone knows that your boss, the CEO, is a bully and ruthless in how he treats those who don't agree with him. Many talented colleagues have resigned but no one addresses the issue for fear of upsetting him.
- Your company's acquisition of a competitor is straining resources and there's no evidence that the forecast cost savings will materialize. Everybody is keeping quiet so as not appear too negative and critical of what was a popular strategic purchase.
- Many of your management colleagues are worried about your company's recent move to outsource some of the manufacturing and are concerned about the impact on product quality and delivery times. The issue is not being openly spoken about because the entire management had originally agreed to this move. No one is willing to admit they may have been wrong.

No matter how uncomfortable, sensitive, sacrosanct or long-running issues may be, successful leaders never leave them brushed under the carpet. They recognize when a topic must be spoken about and resolved, even if this will upset people or create tensions.

Search for elephants in any new roles you take on

Keep your eyes open for any issues within your own team and work environment that may have been left untouched by your predecessor, such as:

- The second-in-command in your team has been under-performing and should have been fired many months ago.
- Your team is split into two camps with obvious tensions and poor collaboration that no one has addressed.

These topics should be relatively easy for you to tackle, given that you're new and want to establish your leadership credentials and authority.

Confirm what is real

Take time to investigate whether the issue is as it appears. Heresay and gossip may be totally untrue and you would have wasted your time and credibility in tackling the supposed problem if you'd waded in without checking things out first.

Openly acknowledge the problem

When you have confirmed the issue is real, talk about it with colleagues and ask them to share their opinions and feelings. Be mindful that some colleagues may feel guilty for causing the issue in the first place or for not have already brought it up and resolved it. Reassure them that your focus is primarily on to solving the issue, rather than to look back, find fault and apportion blame.

Go to the heart of the issue

Make time to fully explore the issue, allowing everyone impacted and involved to speak up and share. Together, agree how to resolve things and move on. There may be situations where you do need to find fault and apportion blame. In such cases be firm and ready to make the tough calls when you realize that somebody might need to be told off, demoted or even have their contract terminated.

LET GO OF THINGS YOU NO LONGER NEED

'Don't be blinded by nostalgia. Clear away that deadwood.'

Is it time for a spring clean to clear out ideas, people, goals and processes that are no longer helping you or your business to succeed? This may include:

- Staff with unhealthy mindsets who are resistant to your leadership or who constantly speak badly of everyone they work with
- Plans and goals that have been important for your business in the past but are past their sell-by dates
- Team members who are not capable of fulfilling their duties and are holding back others who are relying upon them to perform
- Outdated processes and systems that work but might be slow, liable to breakdown or lack the latest functionality and benefits.

After many years in leadership positions, you'll hopefully have learnt through trial and error to never hold on to anything that is not serving you, but when you're new to leadership you may lack the experience and confidence to act as quickly as you should. Try to gain this as soon as possible.

In addition, knowing that you need to let go of something may be the easy bit. Actually doing the letting go can be the challenge, particularly given our tendency to remain in our comfort zones and not wanting to upset others.

Weigh up the pros and cons of updating systems

As soon as you become aware of an outdated system, process or procedure, talk about this with your colleagues and have someone assess how it might need to be updated or replaced. If it will cost money to change, involve your finance team as well, by asking them to carry out a cost-benefit analysis to judge whether the benefits of changing outweigh the up-front and ongoing costs.

Revamp your offices

The same thinking should be applied to buildings such as your offices, warehouses and plants as well as to equipment such as company cars and computers. A run-down and dilapidated office with a terrible layout of rooms and workstations may seem too expensive to renovate. It may, though, be worth it – the benefits in terms of improved staff productivity and motivation from working in a more modern and healthier office layout could more than justify the costs of renovation.

Never hold onto the wrong people

Stop worrying about upsetting an employee who may not be fitting in and focus instead on following your company's HR processes. Give the individual an opportunity to improve (over an agreed timeframe). If they fail to do so, let them go. Be honest with them and try to be as fair as possible with the terms of their contract termination. Explain to the rest of your team why you have taken the decision to fire their colleague. Most of the time, they will have probably been expecting it and wonder what's taken you so long!

Assess the relevance of all ideas and goals

In your team meetings and other discussions, adopt the regular habit of asking colleagues how relevant and valid any of the key assumptions, ways of working, goals and targets are. Decide together which should be scrapped or changed.

THERE'S NO TIME FOR DELAY

'Don't catch the disease of always putting off what should be done today.'

When you procrastinate and put off important decisions and tasks for later, you're not only affecting your own productivity and efficiency but also detrimentally impacting your team. In a 2018 study reported in the *Journal of Occupational and Organizational Psychology*, a team led by two University of Exeter academics found that procrastinating managers make their staff frustrated and less committed to their work. Many staff started to exhibit unhealthy behaviours such as taking extra sick leave, being abusive to colleagues or even stealing office supplies.

Far too many leaders delay working on a task, solving a problem or making a decision for a variety of interconnected reasons:

- Being busy and distracted by other things that are competing for their time and attention
- Not being interested or motivated to spend time on that particular issue
- Not being in the mood and lacking the drive and push to get started
- Assuming it will be easier to do later when the impending deadline will push them to complete the work
- Feel it's too complicated or difficult and decide to simply ignore it.

Not all procrastination is a bad thing. You might recall in chapter 52 the benefits for leaders of slowing down to pause, reflect and make sense of issues and problems facing them. Successful leaders understand the difference between knowing when to take their time with certain issues while also knowing when particular tasks need to be focused on right now.

Even if you enjoy procrastinating about urgent work and burning the midnight oil the night before a report is due, remember that your team may not share your last-minute style. If you want to motivate and inspire them, stop procrastinating.

Get to the root of your problem

When tempted to delay or put something off, stop and ask yourself if you really want to give in to this urge. It may be hard particularly if:

- Your personality lends itself to procrastination, for example you're prone to being slow and reflective and to avoiding tasks.
- You need to overcome any fears holding you back from getting started, such as fear of not doing a good job, struggling or failing.

These might be very deep-seated habits but you can change them with some focus, willpower and determination. If you find it really difficult, find a therapist or coach who can help change these patterns of behaviour using a well-known process called cognitive behavioural therapy (CBT). You can complete this in a few weeks or months, through a series of one-on-one conversations.

Brush up your to-do list and eliminate distractions

To help change your procrastination habit:

- At the end of each working day, tick off what you have accomplished on your to-do list and create a fresh or updated version, listing the important tasks to work on tomorrow. The following morning, make sure you work on the activities you have listed.
- Minimize any distractions that might make it easier for you to procrastinate. What distracts you regularly? Constantly checking your social media or emails? Allowing people to constantly interrupt you? Spending too much time in unproductive meetings?

...but thinking is not procrastination!

Remember to occasionally make time to stop what you're doing and to reflect and consider how you'll deal with your many leadership issues. This might appear to others as if you're procrastinating but you know that this is not the case.

PREPARE FOR THE IMPOSSIBLE

'Beware of writing off the improbable as being impossible.'

Just because something has never happened does not mean it never will. Recent history is stuffed with highly improbable events actually occurring that have shaken and even destroyed businesses and their leaders' careers:

- Companies such as Enron, Kodak, Carillion, Lehman Brothers and Jamie Oliver's restaurants hitting the wall and going bankrupt overnight. If these were a key supplier or client, their closure could have been devastating to your own business.
- Natural disasters such as forest fires, earthquakes, volcanic eruptions and hurricanes, which can have devastating impacts such as widespread loss of life, destroying communities, stopping production, closing airports and cutting off communications – events that can cause your own business major difficulties.

Each of these events may be unexpected but they do seem to be happening with increasing regularity. Successful leaders recognize this and are learning to prepare and plan for these 'black swan' events, named after the discovery that not all swans are white, which was something deemed impossible until Europeans saw one when they first landed in Australia.

Stop being taken by surprise

Accept that the impossible happens and, in some cases, is becoming commonplace. Start being proactive to understand what may occur by carrying out 'what if' analyses. This involves exploring highly improbable but possible scenarios of events that could have a catastrophic impact on your business, such as:

- How would you cope with your main raw material supplier closing down?
- What could you do if your main export markets become closed due to a military coup or major earthquake?
- How would we adjust if the government changed hands and all of our tax incentives were cancelled?
- How do we continue serving our clients if our main factory were totally flooded by the nearby river?

For each possible event, map out how you would help your company to not just survive but thrive.

Get actively involved in risk management

Implement necessary measures to minimize the potential impact of any black swan event. You could think about diversifying your production locations, supplier base or even client base.

Make sure that your business has sufficient insurance coverage for any possible disruptions to your business. Consider having 'key man' insurance for the possibility that you or other key leaders die or become incapacitated. You could even introduce a rule that the leadership team and yourself must never fly on the same flight together to avoid a one in a million chance that you all lose your lives at the same time.

LEAD REMOTE TEAMS CAREFULLY

'The saying 'out of sight, out of mind' has a lot of truth to it when leading people.'

Your leadership skills will be tested the day you're given a globally dispersed team to manage and you no longer have your team sitting happily within earshot of your office door. Having team members in different parts of the country, or even spread over many continents, presents you with a unique set of challenges:

- You can't just sit down with them for a coffee whenever there's something to discuss or if you simply want to catch up.
- You may have team members living in different time zones, reducing the number of hours that both of your working days will overlap. If you're in London and have staff in Hong Kong and San Francisco, you need to fit in early morning calls with those in Asia and late afternoon calls with those in the States. For much of your own working day, you need to get used to the fact that much of your team will be at home asleep.
- You can't pass by their workstations sensing how they are and what they're working on. Instead, you need to manage them while only seeing them on video conference screens or listening to them on the phone.
- Any remotely located staff may feel neglected and forgotten, particularly if you rarely travel to their location and they rarely visit you. As a result, they may easily become demotivated and disengaged.
- If they report to you as well as to a locally based line manager, you may find that your influence is diminished compared to the local manager who probably has a regular face-to-face relationship with them.

Successfully leading remotely located staff involves acknowledging and overcoming these challenges. To do so, you'll need to change your approach to your day-to-day role of connecting and working with your team.

Select remote staff carefully

If you get to choose who in your team will be remotely located, select somebody with the ideal mindset – comfortable working alone and independently, and someone self-driven who won't need constant support and confirmation they are doing the right thing. The ideal candidate is someone who has already worked alongside you so that you both already understand each other's working styles and personalities.

Give them special care and attention

Remote staff need extra care and attention. You can't simply treat them exactly the same way as staff based in your own office. You need to try harder to make them feel valued and equal members of your team:

- Call them on the spur of the moment to ask how things are and just to chat, ideally via a video call so that you can see each other. By doing so, you're trying to mimic the casual and informal connecting that happens in your office when you pass by someone's workstation or meet them in the corridor.
- Plan your travels so that you visit their location and also bring them to yours whenever possible. Be careful allowing your finance staff to push you to reduce costs by travelling less. In my experience, the cost of a train or airfare and a few nights in a hotel is more than offset by the motivational and productivity benefits of being face to face with one of your remotely located team members.
- Similarly support and encourage your other team members to also be in regularly contact with their remote colleagues. When you have an opportunity to create project teams, have mixes of remotely and non-remotely located staff.

AGE IS JUST A NUMBER

'Imagine having to manage staff 50 years older or younger than you.'

Today's leader must become expert at leading people of all ages, particularly as for the first time in history there are five generations working together at the same time:

- The oldest generation who were born before 1946
- The Baby Boomers who were born between 1946 and 1964
- Generation X born between 1965 and 1976
- The Millennials (also known as Generation Y) born between 1977 and 1997
- The youngest generation born after 1997 and known as Generation Z.

With retirement ages rising and people choosing to work in old age, you could conceivably be managing a team of people aged from 20 up to 80. This is like having grandparents working with their grandkids or even great-grandkids, each with very different life experiences and world views. Leading such a diverse age range presents you with some interesting opportunities and challenges.

When thinking about leading such a diverse age range, we tend to put people into boxes making broad assumptions such as:

- Younger staff hate repetitive tasks, are more agile and impatient for career growth
- Older staff are stuck in their ways, wiser, reluctant to change and harder to motivate.

These assumptions influence how we as leaders recruit, promote, delegate, motivate and work with our colleagues, and also affect how people within a team work and collaborate together. But the evidence shows that our assumptions are wrong. This was confirmed by a 2012 research paper that analysed 20 relevant studies involving nearly 20,000 people and concluded that any differences in performance or working style were attributable to non-age-related factors and were not the result of our common assumptions (young people are faster and keener and so on).

Successful leaders understand this and focus on the benefits of having different generations working together.

Overcome any ingrained generational bias

Adopt an open mind by observing and understanding the mindsets, behaviours and actions of each individual team member. You might be surprised to find any assumptions you had been carrying are just wrong, for example discovering that some younger staff are wise beyond their years while some of their older colleagues are more adaptable and ambitious than peers half their age.

Encourage your colleagues to be equally open-minded and observant. Start by openly talking with your team about their experiences and perceptions of working with people much older or younger than themselves. An anonymous survey may be a good idea to help understand what your team are feeling and experiencing, for example that younger people don't listen to older ones, or that older colleagues seem slow and not interested.

Remove age from the equation

Start ignoring a person's age, or at least treating it as a secondary factor, when making decisions about who is hired, promoted and what responsibilities and opportunities you give people. Focus instead on their strengths, actual performance and potential.

Treat having multiple generations as an asset

Differences are good and you should view having different generations within your team in the same way as you do differing personalities, qualifications or work experiences. Having a mixture is always a good thing. People from different generations will bring unique insights, thinking and experiences – what one person misses or misunderstands, another might understand very well. Encourage your team to grasp this.

MANAGE YOUR BOSS

'Sometimes the person most in need of your leadership is your own boss.'

Managing your boss is just as important as managing your own team. This is called leading upwards. This might sound odd, but to be successful you'll often need your boss to:

- Understand and support your needs and requests
- Hear about and be guided by your suggestions and proposals
- Help you gain needed resources and organizational buy-in
- Act in a similar way to you to reinforce your own actions, for example in being firm with a supplier or apologetic to a key client
- Support you in an internal conflict or misunderstanding
- Give you space or other needed support.

To enable these things, you need to lead your boss well to make sure that their expectations, timeframes, actions and words are optimally aligned with yours. This is the same no matter whether your boss is a line manager, a global CEO or Chairperson of your Board of Directors.

If your boss is very senior, elusive or hard to approach, you might feel uncomfortable leading upwards, but research shows it's worth the effort. A global 2016 study by McKinsey & Co, which surveyed 1,200 Chief Marketing Officers, concluded that to achieve business success it's 50 per cent more important to manage upwards (and also – horizontally – manage your peers) than it is to manage your own team. This correlates with the leaders I coach, many of whom realize that they need to manage their bosses even better than they are doing in order to achieve their own goals and KPIs.

Lead in a non-directive way

Your boss may not take kindly to being told what to do because they're more senior and don't have to listen to your requests. If you're too demanding and directive, you risk them viewing you as arrogant and disrespectful. The solution is to lead them indirectly through a combination of:

- Understanding your boss really well, including knowing when they're receptive to suggestions and knowing what motivates and drives them
- Using your skills of influencing and convincing to have them agree to something that they might ordinarily be inclined to reject
- Warming them up over time to your ideas as opposed to simply asking them point blank to agree with your thinking
- Making them feel that your ideas were actually their own.

If all else fails, you may need to be firm and strong, but only do this when you're sure you have all your arguments and facts in order.

Choose your moments wisely

With your own team members, you're free to direct, guide and delegate to them as frequently as you wish. This is obviously not the case with your boss. Be highly selective about your boss' expectations, understanding and actions.

Manage horizontally

With your peers, avoid being too persistent, pushy and demanding. Unlike your boss, your colleagues are less likely to disagree with you directly. They may instead complain about you behind your back.

NEVER BLATANTLY SHOW OFF

'It's not about blowing your own trumpet.'

No matter how successful you are, avoid bragging, praising and shouting about your good fortune. No one is interested or impressed except you and praising yourself produces no gain except to send a message of 'look at me, I am really great'. Sadly, too many leaders can't stop themselves, partly because they have ambitious, arrogant and cocky A-type personalities and also because they're so used to being right and coming out on top.

When I coach such leaders, I realize that they're addicted to wanting the limelight and tend to think that being quiet and humble is a weakness. This is especially so among male leaders – who also seem to more easily get away with showing off than do their female counterparts. With men, we typically view their bragging as showing confidence while for women the same level of showing off is often labelled as arrogant, reflecting our subconscious expectation that women should be more humble and quieter than men.

Genuinely successful leaders have learnt, often the hard way, that there's no lasting value in being a show off because:

- Success is transient and what goes up may just as easily come down
- Seeking the credit and praise is simply a sign of insecurity and lack of wisdom
- Bragging does not endear you to your colleagues and won't win you friends.

The secret is to find the ideal balance between showing confidence versus being humble, while also sharing the successes of you and your team in the best way you can.

Don't be on autopilot

Observe yourself – do you have a pattern of behaviour that you're addicted to and needs to change? Perhaps you're guilty of always remaining quiet and humble and never speaking up or of acting cocky, overconfident and always showing off.

Find your happy medium

You need to practise and develop the skill of knowing when to be humble, be confident or to show off about yourself and/or your team. As a rule of thumb:

- **Be quiet and humble** when the work of your team and yourself speaks for itself and other people already know what has been achieved or when the achievement is standard or small.
- **Act confident** all the time but without becoming arrogant. You can achieve this by balancing your confidence with moments when you admit you're wrong, don't understand something or are unsure of what to do.
- **Share about your own successes** in an understated and low-key manner and only on a selective basis. It's far better that your boss and your internal clients and colleagues speak highly of your work, enabling you to stay quiet.
- **Share about your team's successes** regularly. With your team you're allowed to show off and sing their praises in order to give them visibility and to motivate them. Your intention, however, should never be to indirectly shine the light on you as their boss.

CREATE AN AMAZING WORKING CULTURE

'You are not an Island and it isn't enough to simply focus on becoming an excellent leader.'

A truly successful leader is one who develops a really positive and healthy working culture. Much like the culture we explored in chapter 78, a working culture describes the many ways in which colleagues interact, communicate and work together and the environment that develops as a result.

Poor working culture	Outstanding working culture
• People are scared to speak up • No one challenges their boss • People rush to criticize others and rarely offer compliments • There's no flexi-time or working from home allowed • A strict dress code is enforced • There's an expectation that everyone will work unpaid overtime and take work home at weekends • All staff promotions are based on years of service.	• People openly communicate • Line managers are approachable and used to being challenged • Colleagues regularly thank and complement each other • Staff can sometimes work from home and can dress how they wish, except when meeting clients • A lot of effort is invested in creating work-life balance • There's a feeling that hard work is rewarded and job promotions are based on performance.

Ensuring a positive working culture can be a daunting task because:

- You're not the only leader in your organization, and each of you may have different views and opinions about what makes a good working culture.
- One employee might love the working culture while another might find it stifling or depressing – not everyone values the same things.
- If a CEO is pushing things in a one direction, it can be hard to successfully pull in another.

Walk away from a bad working culture

Never remain in an organization that has a horrible working culture that you believe is never going to get better, no matter how hard you might try. Staying on will only demotivate and depress you and you'll struggle to flourish as a leader. Try to only work in companies where you:

- Enjoy the working culture and feel that you can flourish and succeed
- Sense that the working culture needs to improve and are confident that, with your help, it can develop into one that is more motivating and inspiring.

Audit the working culture

Work with your HR colleagues to conduct annual or bi-annual employee engagement surveys. Use an online survey for this, which allows staff to anonymously answer a broad array of questions that cover all aspects of the working environment. Analyse the results to help you understand the positive and not so positive aspects of the working culture.

In addition, whenever you have an opportunity, have a face-to-face catch up with your staff and seek their ideas for improvement by asking them: 'What do you like and dislike about working here?'. The same question can be posed in the exit interviews of staff who have resigned.

Make a plan of action

Decide what key changes are required to help turn your working culture into one that everybody will agree is outstanding, positive and highly motivating, and draw up an action plan. Involve your leadership colleagues and bosses in this process, reminding them that as leaders everything that each of you do or say has an impact on the working culture.

At least once a month, devote time in a management meeting to review how well you're all doing in role modelling the ideal working culture and working styles. Ask each leader to share success stories to inspire and enthuse each other.

BE THE REAL AUTHENTIC YOU

'Be yourself, no matter what they say.'

As you draw to the end of this book's 100 lessons, it's time to step up, find your leadership voice and become the unique leader that only you're capable of becoming.

No one else is you – with your combination of values, personality, communication style, work experience, strengths, ambitions and dreams. So resist the temptation to take the shortcut of imitating other people such as your role models, bosses and mentors, or to simply apply all of this book's advice without allowing for your own context and needs.

Better to struggle or even fail being your authentic self (as a leader) than to copy someone else's leadership vision, goals or style and to become a half version of what you could be. This would be as unsatisfying and unproductive as owning a BMW sports car with a non-BMW engine (that came from a second-hand family sedan). You would never be able to drive yourself to your full potential.

Successful leaders know that being their true selves ensures that they will be as efficient, effective, energized and inspired as they possibly could be in their leadership roles.

Work hard to find your authentic leadership style

To lead as the real and authentic you means becoming comfortable in your own (leadership) skin and getting over any sense that you're not suitable or worthy of being an outstanding leader. This is the imposter syndrome that we talked about in chapter 53. If you have difficulty in overcoming it, consider seeking the help of a coach or therapist.

Becoming the real you also means finding out what works for you and what doesn't. Do this by continually observing yourself and keeping notes about what you realize, such as:

- If you're not an aggressive and extrovert type of person, think twice before trying to act that way as a leader
- If the values of your boss don't resonate with you, don't act as if they are also your own
- If you feel it doesn't work to delegate as much work as your staff or boss continually suggest you should, create your own optimal delegation plan.

In addition, do learn from mentors, coaches, leaders, books, courses and experts and so on but never totally imitate what they have done. Take only what seems helpful and carefully apply it to your own unique context and needs.

Don't hide your weaknesses

Part of being real and authentic is to discover that you're not perfect and that it's better to be open and transparent about your imperfections and weaknesses. They're as much part of you as your strengths and positive qualities, and to deny the former diminishes who you are.

STEP DOWN BEFORE BEING PUSHED

'We all have an expiry date.'

Far too many leaders overstay their welcome and hang onto to their positions beyond the period in which they were most effective and impactful. This hanging on can result in:

- Their vision, thinking and style turning stale and old-fashioned
- Becoming stubborn and unwilling to listen, adapt and change
- Their support and following declining amongst their colleagues
- Turning lazy and corrupt in both their thinking and their actions
- Potential successors giving up waiting and resigning
- The business or company struggling and losing direction.

It's understandable that a leader may stay on given that power can be addictive. Leadership positions can be enjoyable and have considerable perks, and reaching a leadership position might be pinnacle of someone's career – there may be nothing else they wish to move onto. In addition, we do value leaders with staying power who remain in their roles through various changes, strategy and budget cycles and so on.

There's no magic number or formula to help know when you may have overstayed your welcome, although a 2013 Harvard Business Review reported study calculated that the optimal tenure of a CEO is 4.8 years. This correlates with my own observations that an ideal length for staying in a leadership role is between three and five years depending on the role's level of seniority.

As well as not over-staying, successful leaders also know the importance of leaving on a high when things are going well rather than when they're fired, forced to resign or not re-appointed (when on a fixed term contract). Such ignominious departures are common with well-known examples including the UK's former Prime Minister Margaret Thatcher, the former head of Nissan, Renault and Mitsubishi Carlos Ghosn, Steve Jobs after his first stint as Apple's CEO and Uber's former CEO Travis Kalanick.

Read the signs

Take an annual reality check to assess whether and for how long you wish to continue in your current role. Ask yourself:

- To what degree am I still needed and valued by my bosses and colleagues?
- What will I contribute and create in the year ahead?
- Am I still feeling keen, energetic and passionate about being in this role?
- Do I have things I still want to learn and achieve in this role?
- Are there any danger signs that I need to be aware of that might be a problem for me (e.g. in terms of lacking a sense of direction or becoming stale, or of other people tiring of my style or starting to fall out with me)?
- What other opportunities await me and is now the time to move on?

Talk in confidence with a trusted colleague, friend or executive coach to share your thinking and listen to their opinion. Nobody else can tell you what to do but they can help you sense-check what you're thinking, which should give you the confidence to make your own decision about whether to continue in your role or to plan to resign or retire and move on.

Leave gracefully

When you have decided to move on, plan your departure well:

- Update your CV and quietly job-hunt. Only resign once you have secured a new leadership role because it's so much easier to impress new employers and be offered a new opportunity while you're still employed.
- Spend time choosing and preparing a successor, helping them to be ready to take over when you leave. This topic is covered in the next chapter.
- Be willing to work your entire notice period to help the company transition smoothly. However, if you're in a senior or sensitive leadership position you may be asked to leave immediately.
- Leave your company positively and later always speak highly of your time there as well as of your bosses and colleagues.

HAND OVER THE BATON

'Only a foolish leader walks away from a position with no one in place to continue the good work.'

Although most leaders know that succession planning is really important, they rarely do it well. As a result too many leaders are promoted, resign or retire without having suitably prepared candidates ready to take over. Many of my coaching clients are eager to find and groom potential successors, particularly if they felt under-prepared when moving into their current leadership role.

Knowing who your successor will be, and having them ready to take over from you, has very clear benefits:

- You can spend time preparing and involving them in your daily work as well as helping them understand your vision and strategic thinking.
- Your successor can carry your torch forward in terms of maintaining your working culture, vision, values and strategic direction.
- The formal handing over of your responsibilities will be straightforward and smooth, rather than in a rush over just a few days.
- Your staff, and other stakeholders, can be informed and become used to who will replace you. This is more motivating for them than simply learning the name of their new boss on the day of your departure, or having the position vacant while your successor is found.

Succession planning can be challenging for a number of reasons:

- Evaluating people is not easy and some organizations have weak performance management systems, which makes it harder to objectively choose who may be most suitable.
- There may be no one suitable, because of poor hiring, training and development or because a leader has avoided developing someone in order to make themselves indispensable (i.e. having a mentality of 'you can't fire me because I am the only one capable of running the department').
- Reluctance to inform people they're not potential successors, so that no one candidate is ever singled out and given the needed individual development and exposure.

Be OK if a team member is better than you

If you have a team member who is capable of replacing you, view this as a positive outcome of your successful leadership. You'll be able to delegate much of your work to this person, which leaves you to be more strategic and reflective, while also having more time to motivate and engage your team and to pick up on issues that may otherwise be neglected.

Plan ahead and be objective

Working with your HR colleagues, outline an objective, transparent succession planning process. Ensure that the data from your annual performance appraisal processes is clearly and objectively agreed and recorded, as this will be the basis of your succession planning decisions. In particular, objectively agree with your staff:

- Their KPIs, goals and performance ratings
- Their performance and their potential to take on new responsibilities
- Their motivations, career goals and aspirations.

Be open and transparent with:

- The entire team about when your own position may become vacant
- Your named successor in terms of filling any gaps in their experience, skills and behaviours to enable them to eventually be promoted
- Those who may be hoping to be promoted into your role but you know are not ready. Be honest, even if your feedback might upset them.

Be careful about having a 'may the best man win' mindset and encouraging two or more people to compete against each other. This is a waste of energy, rarely ends well and can create competing camps within the team. It's much better to choose one as your successor and to develop or find suitable future roles within your organization for the others.

KEEP LEADING

'Once a leader, always a leader.'

Successful leaders don't stop leading when they pack up and leave their office for the day. They want to make a difference by bringing their leadership skills to:

- Helping lead a charity or local community organization
- Becoming elected onto the local town or county council
- Being on the Board of Governors or Board of their children's school
- Facilitating family issues such as setting up a trust fund
- Organising the scouts or girl guides in their town
- Being appointed as a non-executive director of a local business
- Becoming active in helping run a local church, mosque or synagogue
- Sitting on their university alumni association committee
- Running a residents' committee or association.

Leaders might take on these paid or pro-bono roles in their evenings and weekends, as well as when they have retired from full-time careers. The benefits to you as a leader when you use your leadership skills in these ways are very important (particularly in retirement):

- Keeping your brain and body active at weekends and in retirement
- Gaining immense fulfilment and satisfaction in providing pro-bono leadership help and seeing the impact of your efforts
- Having a renewed sense of purpose and meaning coming from being of value beyond simply the day job you hold (or held).

It's now time for you to work out how you can give back and provide leadership within your community during your spare time or retirement.

If you can help, then help

You may feel tired and drained after a full week in the office and reluctant to put up your hand to be a leader in your weekends. This is totally understandable but ask yourself whether you're content to do nothing and to simply:

- Send your children to a school which faces all kinds of challenges and yet not wish to help by standing for the school board
- Attend church or mosque each week aware of the financial issues facing the local parish or Muslim community and simply do nothing to help
- Contribute money to a local charity but repeatedly turn down requests to join their board.

As a minimum, use your leadership skills to give back in a small way and offer your help on a one-off or ad hoc basis:

- To a local charity to help restructure its governance framework
- A church to help carry out a fundraising initiative to be able to build a new clock tower
- To teach leadership skills and mentor unemployed young adults for one term at your local community centre.

Lead in retirement

If you're close enough to retiring, explore how you might use your leadership experience and wisdom once you're no longer in a full-time role. As well as keeping you active and engaged, you may well enjoy the new challenges of leading in totally new working environments and organizations.

LEAVE A SUSTAINABLE LEGACY

'The true measure of your greatness comes from what is left when you have gone.'

It's not enough to have simply been a remarkable leader who your former staff fondly remember, you also need to ensure that the positive impact of your leadership remains in place long after you have moved on. In other words, what you create as a leader should be sustainable and ongoing, rather than just a collection of one-off, short-term and momentary successes.

Think of yourself as a leader whose primary task is to plant seeds, water and tend to them, helping them grow into saplings. Long after you have gone, these small plants will have grown into towering trees with deep roots. For truly successful leaders, these metaphorical trees include things like:

- Creating a meaningful vision and mission statement for your company that will continue to guide your colleagues long after you have left
- Being an example and role model who leaves such an impact that your behaviours and mindset are emulated and become part of your company's written core values and unwritten working culture
- Ensuring that your organization has put in place the best practice compliance and ethics guidelines, HR policies and leadership competencies
- Being strategically alert and courageous enough to push your business into future products, markets, technologies and ways of working, and your legacy is leaving a company that continues to prosper long after its competitors may have gone out of business.

Make sure your actions have a positive ongoing impact

Before doing something, always consider the short-, medium- and long-term effects of your actions and choices with the intention that whatever you do is not just for short-term gain but must also be good for the longer term. It might be difficult to precisely know and measure the longer-term impact and longevity of your actions, but you can probably make a good guess and allow this to help determine your choices.

As an example, suppose you're contemplating the introduction of a new process or system that would reduce costs this year but would make it harder moving forward for your team to complete their work within the normal working day and then be forced to work unpaid overtime each week. You might decide not to implement the cost-reducing initiative given the ongoing and longer-term impact on your employees' work-life balance and motivation.

Whenever you face such dilemmas, ask yourself how you want people to remember you. In this example, the choice is simple – between finding ways to cut costs or for helping your team to feel valued, engaged and motivated. How you answer will determine your legacy. Choose wisely.

AND FINALLY...

Be constantly wise, because what you choose to do, think and practice each day is the foundation of the leader you will become.

I genuinely hope that the ideas, exercises and suggestions in this book inspire you to action. I hope that by sharing my own leadership experiences and those of leaders I have coached serves as an amazing guide, equipping you with the tools to succeed on your own leadership journey.

Build on my 100 things. Do your own discovering, learning, experimenting. Create your own list that works for you as a leader.

I would love to keep in touch. Please connect with me on Facebook, LinkedIn, Twitter or Instagram. You can also email me at nigel@silkroadpartnership.com.

REFERENCES

Chapter 6

'Best examples of B2B company mission statements.' The Marketing Blender. Accessed Jan 2020. https://themarketingblender.com/vision-mission-statements/.

Pendell, Ryan. '6 scary numbers for your organization's C-suite.' Gallup. Oct 2018. https://gallup.com/workplace/244100/scary-numbers-organization-suite.aspx.

Chapter 10

Zenger, Jack and Joseph Folkman. 'What great listeners actually do.' *Harvard Business Review*, Jul 2015, https://hbr.org/2016/07/what-great-listeners-actually-do.

Chapter 11

Binder, Carl. 'The six boxes™: A descendent of gilbert's behavior engineering mode.' *Performance Improvement* 37, no. 6 (2007). Accessed May 2019. https://doi.org/10.1002/pfi.4140370612.

Chapter 14

'The Ken Blanchard Companies.' The Ken Blanchard Companies. Accessed Jan 2020. https://kenblanchard.com.

Chapter 17

'Servant leadership.' Wikipedia. Accessed May 2019. https://en.wikipedia.org/wiki/Servant_leadership.

'Robert K. Greenleaf.' Wikipedia. Accessed May 2019. https://en.wikipedia.org/wiki/Robert_K._Greenleaf.

Chapter 21

Friedman, Thomas L. *Thank you for Being Late.* (New York: Farrar, Straus, and Giroux, 2016).

Chapter 22

'The path to IAC® certification.' Certified Coach. Accessed Nov 2019. https://certifiedcoach.org/certification/.

'EMCC competence framework glossary v2.' Accessed May 2019. https://emcc1.app.box.com/s/geavwqnw81rn671xgg6treajoc1xvrnu

Chapter 23

Cameron, Kim, Carlos Mora, Trevor Leutscher, and Margaret Calarco. 'Effects of positive practices on organizational effectiveness.' *The Journal of Applied Behavioural Science* 47, no. 3 (2011): 266-308. Accessed Jan 2020. https://doi.org/10.1177/0021886310395514.

Chapter 27

'Kübler-Ross mode.' Wikipedia. Accessed May 2019. https://en.wikipedia.org/wiki/K%C3%BCbler-Ross_model.

Chapter 28

'2018 Norwest CEO Journey Study.' Norwest Venture Partners. Accessed May 2019. https://nvp.com/ceojourneystudy/.

Chapter 30

Batarseh, Feras A. 'Thoughts on the future of human knowledge and machine intelligence.' *LSE Business Review*, Sept 2017. https://blogs.lse.ac.uk/businessreview/2017/09/20/thoughts-on-the-future-of-human-knowledge-and-machine-intelligence

Rosenbert, Marc. 'Mark my Words: The Coming Knowledge Tusnami.' *Learning Solutions*, Oct 2017. https://learningsolutionsmag.com/articles/2468/marc-my-words-the-coming-knowledge-tsunami.

Chapter 32

Tuckman, B. W. 'Developmental sequence in small groups.' *Psychological Bulletin* 63, no. 6 (1965): 384–399. https://doi.org/10.1037/h0022100

'Bruce Tuckman.' Wikipedia. Accessed June 2019. https://en.wikipedia.org/wiki/Bruce_Tuckman.

Chapter 35

'VIA Character Strengths Assessment.' VIA Institute on Character. Accessed Jan 2020. https://viacharacter.org/.

'Clifton StrengthsFinder.' Gallup. Accessed Jan 2020. https://gallup.com/cliftonstrengths/en/254033/strengthsfinder.aspx.

Chapter 37

Nakano, Chelsi. 'Presentation Habits Presenters Don't Like to Admit.' Prezi Blog. June 2016. https://blog.prezi.com/presentation-habits-presenters-dont-like-to-admit /.

TED: Ideas worth spreading, https://www.ted.com (accessed June 2019)

Chapter 44

Ray, Rebecca L. 'CEO Challenges: Global Leadership Forecast 2018.' DDI, 2018. https://ddiworld.com/glf2018/ceo-challenges.

Caprino, Kathy. 'The Changing Face of Leadership: 10 New Research Findings All Leaders Need to Understand.' *Forbes*, Feb 2018. https://www.forbes.com/sites/kathycaprino/2018/02/28/the-changing-face-of-leadership-10-new-research-findings-all-leaders-need-to-understand/#888b28f61974

Chapter 45

'SMART criteria,' Wikipedia. Accessed May 2019. https://en.wikipedia.org/wiki/SMART_criteria.

Chapter 47

'Sir John Whitmore.' Institute of Coaching. Accessed Jul 2019. https://instituteofcoaching.org/sir-john-whitmore-1937-2017.

Chapter 48

Graves, Laura M. 'Effects of Leader Persistence and Environmental Complexity on Leadership Perceptions: Do Implicit Beliefs Discourage Adaptation to Complex Environments?' *Group Organization and Management* 10, no. 1 (1986): 19-36. https://journals.sagepub.com/doi/pdf/10.1177/105960118501000102

Chapter 56

Niyogi, Shyamalendu. 'Impact of optimist on leadership effectiveness: a review of literature.' *International Journal of Management* 8, no. 6 (2017): 1-8. https://iaeme.com/MasterAdmin/uploadfolder/IJM_08_06_001/IJM_08_06_001.pdf

'Thinking positively about aging extends life more than exercise and not smoking.' YaleNews. Jul 2002. https://news.yale.edu/2002/07/29/thinking-positively-about-aging-extends-life-more-exercise-and-not-smoking

Chapter 58

Garrett, N, SC Lazzaro, D Ariely, and T Sharot. 'The brain adapts to dishonesty.' *Nature Neuroscience* 19, no. 12 (2016). https://www.ncbi.nlm.nih.gov/pubmed/27775721

Chapter 59

Kar-Gupta, Sudip. '"Fatigued" Lloyds CEO takes sick leave.' *Reuters*, Nov 2011. https://uk.reuters.com/article/uk-lloyds/fatigued-lloyds-ceo-takes-sick-leave-idUKTRE7A10Y620111102

Chapter 64

Saporito, Thomas J. 'It's time to acknowledge CEO loneliness.' *Harvard Business Review* (2012). https://hbr.org/2012/02/its-time-to-acknowledge-ceo-lo

Chapter 67

Responsibility assignment matrix. Wikipedia. Accessed Jul 2019. https://en.wikipedia.org/wiki/Responsibility_assignment_matrix

Chapter 69

The World Is Flat. Wikipedia. Accessed Jul 2019. https://en.wikipedia.org/wiki/The_World_Is_Flat

Chapter 73

Thompson, Bryant, and Travis J Simkins. 'Self-oriented forgiveness and other-oriented forgiveness: Shaping high-quality exchange relationships.' *Cambridge University Press Journal of Management and Organization* (2016) https://doi.org/10.1017/jmo.2016.18

Chapter 75

Seiter, Courtney. '7 simple methods to fight against your unconscious biases.' *FastCompany*, Aug 2015. www.fastcompany.com/3044738/7-simple-methods-to-fight-against-your-unconscious-biases

'About the IAT.' Project Implicit. Accessed Jan 2020. https://implicit.harvard.edu/implicit/iatdetails.html

Chapter 78

'Sealed with a kiss: was Obama's smooch in poor taste?' *USAToday*, Nov 2012. https://usatoday.com/story/dispatches/2012/11/20/obama-myanmar-kiss-etiquette-travel/1716667/

'"Lazy Mexicans" Top Gear episode cleared by Ofcom,' *The Telegraph*, Apr 2011. www.telegraph.co.uk/culture/tvandradio/bbc/8426689/Lazy-Mexicans-Top-Gear-episodecleared-by-Ofcom.html

Chapter 86

Peat, Jack. 'More than 25% of UK workers say they have experienced workplace discrimination, survey claims,' *Independent*. Sept 2018. https://independent.co.uk/extras/lifestyle/uk-workers-discrimination-office-workplace-sexismracism-ageism-a8559501.html

Learnlight. 'Learnlight Research Reveals One in Four Employees Has Experienced Workplace Discrimination.' Learnlight Insights. Accessed Jan 2020. https://insights.learnlight.com/en/articles/learnlight-research-reveals-one-in-four-employees-has-experienced-workplace-discrimination/

Parker, Kim and Cary Funk. 'Gender Discrimination comes in many forms for today's working women.' Pew Research Center Fact Tank. Dec 2017. https://www.pewresearch.org/fact-tank/2017/12/14/gender-discrimination-comes-in-many-forms-for-todays-working-women/

'Poll finds at least half of Black Americans say they have experienced racial discrimination in their jobs and from the police.' Harvard TH Chan School of Public Health Press Release. Oct 2017. htpps://.hsph.harvard.edu/news/press-releases/black-americans-discrimination-work-police/

Chapter 89

Workshy bosses breed contempt and abuse in the workforce, research shows. University of Exeter Research News. Sept 2018. https://www.exeter.ac.uk/news/featurednews/title_682831_en.html (Accessed August 2019)

Chapter 92

Costanza, David P., Jessica M. Badger, Rebecca L. Fraser, Jamie B. Severt, and Paul A. Gade. 'Generational differences in work-related attitudes: a meta-analysis.' *Journal of Business and Psychology* 17, no. 4 (2012): 375-395 https://link.springer.com/article/10.1007/s10869-012-9259-4

Chapter 93

Barta, Thomas and Patrick Barwise. 'Why effective leaders must manage up, down, and sideways.' *McKinsey Quarterly*, Apr 2017. https://www.mckinsey.com/featured-insights/leadership/why-effective-leaders-must-manageup-down-and-sideways

Chapter 97

Luo, Xueming, Vamsi K Kanuri, and Michelle Andrews. 'Long CEO Tenure Can Hurt Performance.' *Harvard Business Review*, Mar 2013. https://hbr.org/2013/03/long-ceo-tenure-can-hurt-performance

Chapter 98

Rosenthal, Jeff, Kris Routch, Kelly Monahan, and Meghan Doherty. The holy grail of effective leadership succession. Deloitte Insights. Sept 2018. https://www2.deloitte.com/us/en/insights/topics/leadership/effective-leadership-succession-planning.html